Positively Crochet!

By Mary Jane Hall

©2007 by Mary Jane Hall
Published by

An Imprint of F+W Publications

700 East State Street • Iola, WI 54990-0001
715-445-2214 • 888-457-2873
www.krausebooks.com

Our toll-free number to place an order or obtain a free catalog is
(800) 258-0929.

The following trademarked terms and companies appear in this
publication:

Aleene's® OK to Wash It®, Aunt Lydia's® Quick Crochet Cotton,
Bernat® Galaxy, Bernat® Softee Chunky, Bernat® Super Value,
Berroco® Softwist™, Brown Sheep Company, Inc. Lamb's Pride,
Caron® Rainbow Tones, DMC® Color Variations Embroidery Floss,
DMC Senso Cotton, Hilos Omega Nylon Thread, iPod, J&P Coats®
Knit-Cro-Sheen™ Cotton Crochet Thread, J&P Coats® Royale™ Fine
Crochet, J&P Coats® Speed-Cro-Sheen, Jimmy Beans Wool Nashua
Wooly Stripes, Jo-Ann™ Sensations Angel Hair, Lion Brand® Festive
Fur, Louisa Harding Yarns Sari Ribbon, Noro Kureyon, Offray Ribbon,
Patons® Bohemian, Patons® Classic Wool® Merino, Patons® Grace,
Pellon® Peltex® 70, Plymouth Yarn® Company Inc. Encore, Sinfonia
Cotton, Red Heart® Symphony™, Red Heart® TLC, Swarovski™, TLC®
Cotton Plus™, TLC® Heathers™

Library of Congress Catalog Number: 2007923005

ISBN 13: 978-0-89689-517-1
ISBN 10: 0-89689-517-3

Model shots by Photography by JD, Clintonville, WI
Designed by Rachael Knier
Edited by Erica Swanson

Printed in China

DEDICATION

I want to dedicate this book to my family, but mostly to Almighty God, who has paved the way for me and made all this possible. He has blessed me "beyond my dreams," and I want to honor Him and give Him all the glory for the talents and opportunities He has given me throughout my life. Without God, I would not be able to share the positive thoughts on life that I have shared in this book. He is so awesome! My prayer is that many lives will be touched by my thoughts.

"Delight in the Lord and He will give you the desires of your heart."
Psalms 37:4.

ACKNOWLEDGMENTS

I would like to thank my family and friends who have so lovingly supported me during the writing of this book. I want to give a special thanks to my husband, Terry, for putting up with all of the times I had to give more attention to creating my designs than to our marriage, and to thank him for all the positive and motivating tips I have learned from him over the years through listening to his "Yes You Can" motivational seminars. A special thanks goes to my daughter, Jamie Vaduva, for being my personal assistant, artist, model and "right-hand man," so to speak. Without their support, this book would not have been possible. I also want to thank my sisters, Judy Drewett and Donna Howard, who cheered me on each step of the way and overlooked the times I wasn't my best because of all the pressures and deadlines.

I cannot forget to mention all of the wonderful friends who tested the patterns in this book, giving me peace of mind. I just cannot thank them enough. They helped to keep me sane and made the whole process smoother. A special thank you to: Alyssa Denen, Aminta Moses, Yvonne Bowser, Jackie Brown, Judy Drewett, Anca Hall, Karol Holloway, Pam Frye, Becky Wooly, Judy Morrison, Brandy Arner, Annette Stewart, Nova Carman, Lisa Davis, Adrienne Clark, Pat Tansky, Melody Kelly and Janice Tobe. I must also give a big thank you to Cindy Gillispie, who patiently walked me through the process of putting the final manuscript together before my deadline. I feel indebted to all these wonderful people.

I'd like to acknowledge the models who were photographed for this book: Nicole Short, Shelley Krueger, Kylie Krueger, Abby Olson, Natasha Quaintance, Hannah Miller and Jamie, Jade and Sophia Vaduva. They made my designs look wonderful! I must also thank world-famous Photography by JD's Dave, Jean and JD Wacker for the exceptional job they did with the photographs.

And last but not least, I want to thank my editor, Erica Swanson, Candy Wiza, Rachael Knier, and the entire staff at Krause Publications for believing in me and helping to make this book become a reality.

Table of Contents

INTRODUCTION

If you are a crochet fanatic like me, you know that this is an exciting time for crocheting. Statistics from the Crochet Guild Of America (CGOA) say that there are now more crocheters than knitters in the United States. Crochet is everywhere! I learned to knit years ago, and I love the look of knitting, but crocheting is my passion. Every person I have interviewed who knows how to knit and crochet says that crocheting is faster and more fun. So move over, knitters! We will no longer take a back seat! The world might as well face it — crochet is here to stay.

Crocheting is amazingly easy, and if you are patient enough to learn how to hold the hook and yarn, you can create almost anything. I have taught many people to crochet, and most are thrilled at how easy it is. You'll be amazed at what you can do. All it takes is a couple of hours to practice the basic stitches before you can get your project started. After she learned to crochet, my daughter-in-law, a long-time knitter, literally jumped up and down, saying, "Why didn't you teach me this a long time ago? This is so much fun!"

For this book, I have created more than 50 fabulous and easy-to-crochet projects that you'll be proud to wear. Some patterns even go up to size 3x! You'll be inspired to share your work with others, and you'll find many ideas to get started. All it takes is desire and believing in yourself.

I am also excited to share positive and encouraging tips on life that I hope will be meaningful to you and your family. Sometimes life is fun, just like crocheting, but sometimes life can be very hard (like some crochet). Some of the tips are from my husband Terry, who travels all over the country giving positive-thinking seminars. We have been married for 36 years, and his enthusiasm has rubbed off on me! I hope you'll want to share these tips that mean so much to me with your friends and loved ones.

So what are you waiting for? Get that crochet hook and yarn out, and let's get started!

Mary Jane

BASIC INFORMATION

Stitches Used In This Book:

Chain, slip stitch, single crochet, half-double crochet, double crochet, triple crochet, double treble crochet, cluster stitch, puff stitch, popcorn stitch, clover stitch, shell stitch, bobble stitch, single crochet V-stitch, double crochet V-stitch, picot stitch, circle stitch.

Abbreviations:

approx.	approximately		p	picot
beg	beginning		patt	pattern
bbl(s) st	Bobble(s) stitch		pc	popcorn
blo	back loop only		pm(s)	place marker(s)
CC	contrasting color		prev	previous
ch(s)	chain (s)		rem	remaining
cl	cluster stitch		rep(ing)	repeat(ing)
clo(s) st	clover(s) stitch		rnd(s)	round(s)
cont (ing)	continue(ing)		RS	right side(s)
dc	double crochet		sc	single crochet
dc2tog	double crochet two together		sc2tog	single crochet two together
dec(s)	decrease(s)		sh(s)	shell(s)
dtr	double treble; also quadruple (yarn over three times)		sk	skip
			sl st(s)	slip stitch(s)
fig	figure		sp(s)	space(s)
foll	following		st(s)	stitch(es)
gr(s)	group(s)		tch	turning chain
hdc	half-double crochet		tog	together
2hdctog	two half-double crochet together		tr	triple crochet (yarn over two times)
inc(s)	increase(s)(ing)		V-st	V-stitch
lp(s)	loop(s)		WS	wrong side
opp	opposite		wt	weight
oz.	ounce(s)		yo	yarn over (wrap yarn around hook)

Standard Yarn Weight System:

Yarn Weight Symbol and Category Names	SUPER FINE 1 SUPER FIN Super Fino	FINE 2 FIN Fino	LIGHT 3 LEGER Ligero	MEDIUM 4 MOYEN Medio	BULKY 5 BULKY Abultado	SUPER BULKY 6 SUPER BULKY Super Abultado
Types of Yarns in a Category	Sock, Fingering, Baby	Sport, Baby	DK, Light, Worsted	Worsted, Afghan, Aran	Chunky, Craft, Rug	Bulky, Roving

A Note About Gauge:

Gauge, the measurement of your stitches, is very important, especially when you are making clothing. You do not want your (supposedly) adult-sized sweater to fit a five-year-old! Believe me, it can happen very easily, even if your gauge is only off by a fraction of an inch. Follow the gauge in these patterns closely. Work up a 4" x 4" swatch before beginning any garment, measuring the gauge in the center of the swatch. To do that, place straight pins at the beginning and end of the designated number of stitches (or rows), and then count the number of stitches between the pins. If your gauge does not match, keep trying a larger (or smaller) hook until you get the correct gauge.

Gauge is not quite as important with scarves and purses as with the clothing, but if you want your crocheted project to look exactly like the one in the photo, you need to follow the gauge. Check it often, because when you lay a project down and come back a day, week or month later, your gauge could be quite different.

When substituting a yarn that is the same weight according to the standard yarn weight system, be sure to make a swatch and measure your gauge carefully. Yarns can fool the eye, so don't just go by the substitutions given. Yardage also varies with different yarns, and you may need more or less than the quantity specified in the pattern.

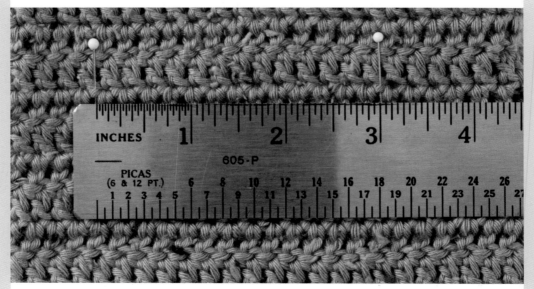

Measure gauge carefully before beginning your project.

Size Chart:

I recommend circling the size you are making on each pattern for less confusion. If you go by these measurements, the garment should fit. Keep in mind that most of the garments in this book will stretch.

Bust (at fullest point):

XS (0-2)	32"-33"
S (4-6)	34"-35"
M (8-10)	36"-37"
L (12-14)	38"-39"
XL (16-18)	40"-41"
1X (18-20)	44"-45"
2X (20-22)	46"-47"
3X (24-26)	48"-49"

To Felt:

Place the project inside a zippered pillowcase, and put it in the washing machine on the hottest, lowest water-level setting. If the water is not hot enough, turn up the heat or pour boiling water into the machine as it fills up. Place tennis shoes in the washer to help with agitation. Add 1 Tbs. detergent and ¼ cup baking soda. You may have to repeat this process 1-3 times, depending on how you want the finished project to look. Placing the piece in a sink with ice water at the end of cycle will help it to felt. Let the piece dry completely. To learn more about felting, read *Felted Crochet* by Jane Davis.

Directions for Striped Bracelet on pg. 15.

To Increase and Decrease:

To increase a sc, hdc or dc: Work 2 sc, 2 hdc or 2 dc in same st.

To work 1 sc decrease (2sctog): Place hook in st, yo and pull through st, with 2 lps on hook, place hook in second st, with 3 lps on hook, yo and pull through all 3 lps.

To work 1 hdc decrease (2hdctog): * Yo, insert hook in next st, yo, pull up a lp * rep from * to * once, yo and draw through all 5 lps on hook.

To work dc decrease (2dctog): Yo, insert hook in st, yo and pull lp through st, yo and pull through 2 lps on hook, yo, insert hook in next st, yo and pull lp through st, yo and pull through 2 lps on hook, yo and pull through all 3 lps on hook.

Skill Level — Intermediate

MEDIUM
4
MOYEN
Medio

Fits sizes xsm-med (lg-xlg, 1x-2x)

Circular Shrug

Dress up this stunning shrug with a sparkling brooch and skirt,
or go for a casual look by leaving it open with a pair of jeans. It may
take awhile to make because of the close single-crochet stitches,
but focusing on the results will energize you!

INSTRUCTIONS:

All hdc are worked in back lp only (blo).

Row 1: Ch 107 (116, 125), hdc in third ch from hook, hdc in next 13 sts (15 hdc), counting ch 3 as first dc. * In next ch, work (sc, ch 1, sc — V-st made), sk 2 ch; rep from * until you have 15 chs left — 26 (29, 32) V-sts. Hdc in rem 15 chs, ch 2, turn. Ch 2 counts as first hdc at beg of each row.

Row 2: Sk first hdc in back lp only, hdc in each of next 14 hdc, * V-st in next ch 1 sp, rep from * to last V-st, hdc (blo) in each of next 15 hdc, end with last hdc in tch, ch 2, turn. (15 hdc, 26 [29, 32] V-sts, 15 hdc.) Measure the width of your work. If it is not 30" (33", 36") wide, changer to a larger or smaller hook.

Rows 3-60 (66, 66): Rep Row 2 or until center measures 21" (23¼", 27"). Sides will be flared. End off.

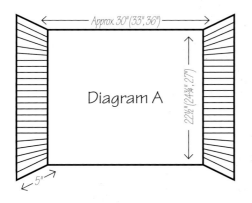

Approx. 30" (33", 36")

Diagram A

22½" (24¾", 27")

5"

Next Step: Underarm Seam — Fold piece and sew 8½" (9", 9½") seam on each side, leaving a 6½" (7½", 8½") open sp (See Diagram B). Try shrug on and make sure armhole is large enough.

Sleeves (optional)

Make 2 — Pm on first st of each rnd.

Note: One side (armhole) is the foundation ch side, and the V-sts will be going in the opposite direction.

Rnd 1: Attach yarn to st at underarm seam. (Sc, ch 1, sc) in same st as joining. * Sc-V-st in next V-st, rep from * around armhole. Join to first sc here and throughout rem rnds on sleeve with sl st — 17 (20, 23) sc-V-sts.

Rnd 2: Ch 1, * V-st in next V-st, rep from * around, join — 17 (20, 23) V-sts.

Rnd 3-10: Rep Rnd 2 — 17 (20, 23) V-sts on each rnd.

Rnd 11 (Dec rnd): Ch 1, 1 sc in first V-st, ch 1, 1 sc in top of next V-st (dec made). V-st in each of next 15 (18, 21) V-sts. 16 (19, 22) V-sts total — Mark first V-st dec.

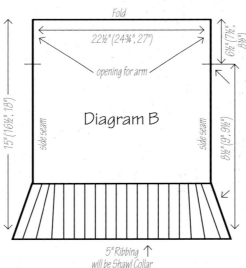

Fold

22½" (24¾", 27")

opening for arm

6½" (7½", 8½")

Diagram B

15" (16½", 18")

side seam

side seam

8½" (9", 9½")

5" Ribbing
will be Shawl Collar

Materials:

4 (5, 6) skeins (3.5 oz./ 100 g/200 yd. each) yarn in plum

Size K/10.5 (6.5 mm) hook

Yarn needle

Used in this project: Plymouth Encore yarn in Mauvetone

Gauge:

3 hdc = 1"

4 hdc (ribbed) rows = 2"

4 sc ribbed rows on cuff = 1¼"

1 V-st = 1"

4 V-st rows = 1½" (each rib section is 5" on each end)

Special Stitch:

Single Crochet V-Stitch (sc-V-st): Sc, ch 1, sc in designated st.

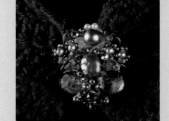

Words of Encouragement

My husband shared this from a seminar he attended once: "When you see results, discipline comes easy!" This can be applied to a crochet project or life. Even if you have not achieved the results you want, try to see the results in your mind. This is the "as if" principle. At age 16, when my daughter was in the Fourth of July Queen pageant, she was competing with many pretty girls. Before she went up on stage, I told her to smile and act as if she had already won. It gave her confidence and energy, and she won! Seeing things in your mind can be very powerful!

Rnd 12: Work 16 (19, 22) V-sts even, remembering to work first V-st in dec at beg — 16 (19, 22) V-sts.

Rnd 13: Rep Rnd 12 — 16 (19, 22) V-sts.

Rnd 14: Dec 1 V-st, as in Rnd 11 — 15 (18, 21) V-sts.

Rnds 15 - 16: Work even with no dec — 15 (18, 21) V-sts.

Rnd 17: Dec 1 V-st as in Rnd 11 — 14 (17, 20) V-sts.

Rnds 18-19: Work even — 14 (17, 20) V-sts.

Rnd 20: Dec 1 V-st, as in Rnd 11 — 13 (16, 19) V-sts.

Rnds 21-22: Work even. End off — 13 (16, 19) V-sts.

Ribbing for Sleeves
The first step is worked in rnds:

With RS facing, attach yarn to sc at RS of sc-V-st at underarm of sleeve.

Ch 1, sc in same st as joining. Skipping over each ch 1, sc in each sc around, attach with sl st to first sc — 26 (30, 34) sc. Remainder of cuff is worked in rows and attached to side of sleeve end.

First Row of Ribbing
All sts are worked in back lp only.

Row 1: Ch 7, turn, sc in back lp in second ch from hook and in each of next 5 chs, sl st in same sp as first ch, sl st in next 2 sc of sleeve, turn. Do not ch 1 — 6 sc on each row of ribbing.

Row 2: Skipping over beg 3 sts, sc in each of next 6 sc, ch 1, turn — 6 sc.

Row 3: Sc in each of next 6 sc, sl st into same st at beg of row, sl st into next 2 sc, turn. Do not ch 1.

Rows 4-26 (30, 34): Rep Rows 2 and 3. Turn sleeve inside-out and sew Rows 1 and 26 (30, 34) of cuff tog with yarn and yarn needle.

Finishing
Weave in ends. If you have holes where you attached yarn to start working sleeves because of a loose beginning ch, unravel a long piece of your yarn and separate 1 ply. Carefully sew the holes up from the WS with a sewing needle and 1 ply of the yarn as your thread for a perfect match.

Helpful Hint:
If you have an extra-large space from a loose stitch in a garment, just sew it together as you would a hole in fabric. Use the same color yarn, and untwist it to use 1-ply as thread.

Skill Level — Advanced Beginner

MEDIUM
4
MOYEN
Medio

Finished size — Approx. 8½" x 8¾", without straps

Fun Circles Bag

Self-striping yarn is used to make this retro bag, so each one you make may turn out differently. The easy 3-D circles are worked right into each row! How cool is that?

Materials:

- 2 balls (100 g/109 yd.) 100% wool hand-painted yarn
- Size I/9 (5.5 mm) and size G/6 (4 mm) hooks
- 1 large snap for closure
- Yarn needle
- ⅓ yd. fabric for lining (optional)
- Sewing needle and thread to match fabric

Used in this project: Noro Kureyon yarn, 100% wool, in color #165.

Gauge:

Body of Purse, with I hook:
- 7 sc = 2"
- 2 sc rows = 1"
- 1 sc Circle = ⅞"

Strap, with G hook:
- 6 sc = 1¼"

Special Stitch:

Circle Stitch — Ch 4, sl st in second ch from hook, 3 sc in each of next 2 ch, join with sl st to first sl st at beg, which will form a circle. Ch 1, flip circle over, and sl st to backside of first sc on circle. Sl st in same sc at base of ch 4 (sl sts are not included in st counts).

INSTRUCTIONS:
Work in rows.

Front
With I hook, ch 29.

Row 1: Sc in second ch from hook and in each ch across, ch 1, turn — 28 sc.

Row 2: Sc in each sc across 28 sc, ch 1, turn — 28 sc.

Row 3: Sc in first 2 sc, * work circle st, sc in next 5 sc; rep from * across row, end with sc in last sc, ch 1, turn — 6 circle sts.

Row 4: Sc in first sc, * sc in st in back of circle st, sc in next 4 sc, rep from *, end with sc in last sc, ch 1, turn — 28 sc.

Rows 5-6: Sc in each sc across, ch 1, turn — 28 sc.

Row 7: Sc in first 4 sc, work circle st, * sc in next 5 sc, circle st; rep from *, end with sc in last 4 sc, ch 1, turn — 5 circle sts.

Row 8: Sc in first 4 sc, sc in st in back of circle st, * sc in next 4 sc, sc in back of circle st, rep from *, end with sc in last 3 sc, ch 1, turn — 28 sc.

Rows 9-10: Sc in each sc, ch 1, turn — 28 sc.

Rows 11-34: Rep Rows 3-10 three more times. End off.

Back
Worked the same as front, omitting circle sts. Ch 29.

Row 1: Sc in second ch from hook and each ch across. Ch 1, turn — 28 sc.

Rows 2-34: Work even in sc — 28 sc. End off after row 34.

Bottom and Side Insert
Row 1: With I hook, ch 5, sc in second ch from hook and in each ch across, ch 1 turn — 4 sc.

Rep Row 1, working 4 sc per row until piece measures 25½" long. End off.

Attaching Insert to Purse Body
With RS tog, pin insert to sides and bottom of front piece, one section at a time, leaving top open. With yarn needle and yarn, sew insert to front using whip st. Rep with other side of insert and back piece. Turn bag RS out.

Strap
Crochet tightly for firmness. With G hook, ch 3.

Row 1: Sc in second ch from hook and in last ch, ch 1, turn — 2 sc.

Cont working sc rows until strap is 29" long. End off. Attach ends of strap to each side at top of bag with yarn needle and yarn using whip st.

Optional Lining: Cut fabric into two pieces, each measuring 9½" (height) x 10½" (width). With RS tog, machine or hand sew ⅓" seams on bottom and two sides, leaving opening at top of short end. Put lining (WS tog) inside bag to make sure it fits. Take out and fold top part of lining over approx. 1". Place inside bag and make adjustments as needed. Pin lining to top edge, and sew to purse with needle and thread. Sew each side of snap to inside of bag at top center for closure.

Weave in ends. If you want the circles to lie flat, sew them down with needle and thread.

Words of Encouragement
If you want to succeed at anything, start having some fun. Dale Carnegie said, "People rarely succeed unless they have fun in what they are doing." I can relate to that, because I never in a million years thought I could get paid for something that I absolutely love to do! My first two years of designing have been wonderful, and I think one reason is because I am having a lot of fun!

Striped Bracelet

This quick and easy project requires absolutely no thinking at all! So call up a friend and share a cup of coffee while you work on this bracelet. The multicolor yarn makes it look like you spent hours placing the stripes side by side, but you can make this project in just two minutes!

Materials:

1 oz. multicolored yarn
(Size and weight
do not matter)
Any size hook
Bangle bracelet, any size

INSTRUCTIONS:

With bracelet in left hand (right hand if you are left-handed), place hook in center of bracelet, grab the slip knot with hook, and bring back through center of bracelet, working around bracelet, sc. Cont working sc around bracelet, completely covering it with yarn. Join to first sc with sl st. End off. Push raised part of sc to inside of bracelet.

Words of Encouragement

Some of my favorite things in life are the smell of a scented candle and the aroma of a good cup of coffee. Even better though, is a pleasant chat with a friend. What about your family? Is your speech as a pleasant, lingering aroma to them, or do your words have a bitter aftertaste? You can always add some sugar for sweetness. A little sugar never hurt anyone!

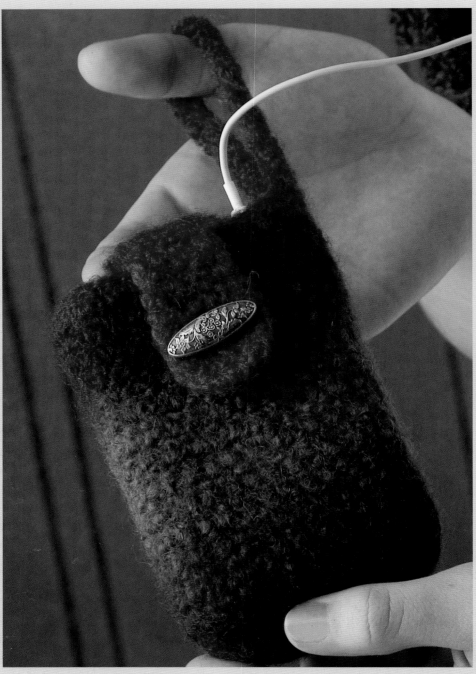

Skill Level — Beginner

Size before felting: 4½" x 6½", size after felting: 3" x 5"

Felted iPod Cozy

This popular cozy would also make a great cell phone case! You'll love the way the colors blend with this yarn, and the case even has a pocket for your earbuds. If you are unhappy with the results, keep putting it through the wash until it is the right size.

INSTRUCTIONS:

Bottom

Row 1: Ch 13, sc in second ch and in each ch across, ch 1, turn each row — 12 sc.

Rows 2-3: Sc in each sc across. Do not end off — 12 sc.

Body

Ch 2, hdc in same sp (inc), do not turn, cont around short end, working hdc in each st, 2 hdc in each corner and 1 hdc on each short end, sl st to ch 2 — 30 hdc.

Rows 2-15: Cont working in rnds, sl st to ch 2 at end of each row. End off — 30 hdc.

Tab

Row 1: With back facing, mark 6 sts at center top edge, attach yarn to first marked st, ch 2 (first hdc) hdc in next 5 hdc, ch 2, turn — 6 hdc.

Rows 2-8: Hdc in each st — 6 hdc.

Row 9: Work 2hdctog (to dec, see pg 9) at beg and end of row. End off — 4 hdc.

Strap

Attach yarn to side top edge at fold, ch 37, sl st to next st, ch 1, turn; sl st in each ch across and to top edge. End off — 37 sl sts.

Pocket

Row 1: Ch 13, hdc in third ch (ch 2 counts as first st) and each ch across, ch 2, turn — 12 hdc.

Rows 2-11: Hdc in each st. End off after Row 11 — 12 hdc.

Sew pocket to back of cozy with yarn and yarn needle. Weave in ends.

Use the pocket to store earbuds or cash.

To Felt

See pg 9. This cozy was put through the wash cycle twice. Stretch the strap when wet to fit around your wrist. Sew button to tab, and sew a snap to the underside of tab.

Cozy before and after felting

Words of Encouragement

Are you unhappy with the way your life has turned out? Do you want the next 10 years of your life to turn out differently? The best time to make that happen is now! You can control your destiny by making a decision this moment to say and do things that will make the next 10 years better and happier.

Helpful Hint:

If you are looking for design ideas, ask little girls what they like. You'll be surprised at what they say!

Fits sizes xs-med (lg-xlg, 1x-2x)

Easy Shrug

·This is one of the easiest garments you will ever make. A single crochet is used to make this shrug, which is crocheted into a "T" shape, then side seams are sewn to form a circular shape. You can wear the shrug open, or bring the front together and pin with a pretty brooch.

INSTRUCTIONS:

Entire shrug is worked in back loop only (blo).

Ch 37 (40, 43) loosely.

Row 1: Sc in second ch from hook and in each ch across, ch 1, turn — 36 (39, 42) sc.

Rows 2-57 (59, 61): In blo, sc in each sc across row — 36 (39, 42) sc.

Next Step: At end of Row 57 (59, 61), do not ch 1 and do not turn piece. Do not end off. Ch 37 (40, 43) for back. Turn.

Row 58 (60, 62): Sc in second ch from hook and in each ch, cont to work scs to end of row, ch 1, turn — 72 (78, 84) sc.

Rows 59-114 (61-118, 63-122): Sc in each sc across — 72 (78, 84) sc.

Row 115 (119, 123): Sc (blo) 36 (39, 42) sc in each of next 36 (39, 42) sc, ch 1, turn.

Rows 116-171 (120-177, 124-183): Sc (blo) in each of next 36 (39) sc — 36 (39) sc across, ch 1, turn. Do not ch 1 at end of last row. End off.

Side Seams

Following diagram, sew A to B, leaving an armhole opening at C. Try shrug on for fit, having seams in back, below armhole opening, and turning over long edge (D) for shawl collar. If armhole is too big, sew tog several ridges at armhole to fit, starting at side seam. Weave in ends.

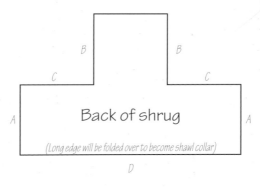

B   B

C   C

A   **Back of shrug**   A

(Long edge will be folded over to become shawl collar)

D

Materials:

3 (3, 4) skeins (5 oz./ 140 g/260 yd. each) 3-ply worsted-wt. yarn in green

Size K/10.5 (6.5 mm) hook

Yarn needle

Used in this project: TLC Red Heart Yarn in Dark Sage

Gauge:

12sc and 16 rows = 4"

16 rows = 4"

Words of Encouragement

Is there someone in your life who always sees your faults and can never find anything nice to say? Usually these people are insecure about themselves and want to bring you down to lift themselves up; but nobody wants to be around a cactus, and it hurts to be with someone who is critical all the time. Try not to focus on how they make you feel or the negative things in their lives. My husband always says, "Give them what they need, not what they deserve."

Helpful Hint:

Since entire shrug is worked in the back loop only, it will stretch to fit all sizes.

Button Bracelet

One size fits all

Skill Level — Beginner

Materials:
26-30 decorative buttons with eyes in the back
Elastic thread
Size D/3 (3.25 mm) hook

INSTRUCTIONS:
Place buttons onto elastic in desired order. Make slip knot, leaving a 6" tail. Pull up first button, and ch 1 loosely around it; rep with remaining buttons to fit around wrist. End off and tie ends tog.

These black and brass bracelets are created with simple chains, and they are easy enough for a child to make. There's no right or wrong way to make this beautiful project!

Delicate Charm Necklace

Materials:
24-gauge wire
Size B/1 (2.25 mm) hook
8 charms
9 black faceted glass beads
1 jewelry closure

INSTRUCTIONS:
Place charms and beads onto wire in desired order. Leaving a 6" tail, ch 26, * pull up a bead and ch around it, ch 1, pull up a charm and ch around it; rep from * to last bead, ch 26. End off, leaving a 6" tail.

Closure
Place 1 end of tail into small circle that is on 1 end of closure, and pull close to ch. Weave end of wire through ch and small circle 2-3 times to secure; rep on other end.

Finished length — 18"   Skill Level — Beginner

Words of Encouragement
Do you always have to be right? Does your pride stop you from ever admitting that you're wrong? It won't kill you to be wrong! What about your relationship? Do you constantly argue to prove your point? You might want to ask yourself, "Do you want to be happy, or do you want to be right?"

Skill Level — Beginner

MEDIUM
4
MOYEN
Medio

Size before felting — 8½" x 96", size after felting — 5½" x 60"

One-Skein Felted Scarf

Felted crochet is hot right now, and this quick project will show off your skills. When you want to felt any item, make sure that you use 100-percent natural animal fibers or yarn that is meant for felting. Man-made fibers will not felt, but they can be added as an accent. Once you start felting, you will love it!

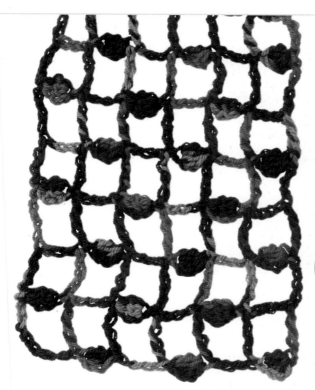

Scarf before and after felting.

INSTRUCTIONS:

Ch 27.

Row 1: Ch 7, in thirteenth ch from hook, work 1 dtr, * ch 3, work cl st in first ch of ch 3, sk 3 chs, dtr in next ch, ch 3, sk 3 chs, dtr in next ch, rep from *. End with cl st, dtr in last ch/st, turn — 7 dtr, 6 sps and 3 cl sts.

Row 2: Ch 6 (first dtr) * ch 3, sk next cl, dtr in next dtr, ch 3, cl in first ch of ch 3, dtr in next dtr, rep from *, after last cl st, sk 3 chs, dtr in next ch, turn — 7 dtr, 6 sps, 3 cl sts.

Rows 3-52: Rep Row 2. After last row, end off.

To felt scarf, see pg 9. Lay flat to dry.

Materials:

1 skein (3.5 oz/223 g) variegated 100% wool yarn (or other natural fiber that will felt)

Size K/10.5 (6.5 mm) hook

Yarn needle

Used in this project: Patons Classic Wool Merino in Harvest

Gauge:

4 dtr (w/ sps between) = 4½"

2 dtr rows = 4"

Special Stitch:

Cluster Stitch (cl st): Yo, insert hook in first ch, yo, draw through 2 lps on hook (3 times), yo and draw through 4 lps on hook.

Double Treble Crochet (dtr) (also called quadruple): Yo 3 times, insert hook into st, draw up lp (5 lps on hook), yo and draw through 2 lps, 4 times.

Helpful Hint:

If you are a beginner, don't choose an afghan as your first project. It will take a long time to finish, and you may get discouraged and quit. Start with an easy project, such as a scarf, so you can see quick results.

Words of Encouragement

Are you good at not only loving, but showing love as well? There are many people who have a hard time bringing themselves to say those three little words: "I love you." If you love someone, you shouldn't just assume that they know — say it. I have a friend whose husband never says, "I love you." I heard him say to her, "Well, I told you I loved you when I married you. If I ever change my mind, I'll let you know!" He thought that was being clever, but it hurt my friend. Learning to say the words will build self-esteem and make your loved ones feel secure.

Finished size — 12½" x 7", without handles

BULKY
5
BULKY
Abultado

Sari Silk Purse

Sari silk yarn is interesting and unique, but it can be challenging to work with because of its many inconsistencies. Just don't give up. With patience, your project will be beautiful and bursting with color!

INSTRUCTIONS:
Work in rounds.

Rnd 1: Ch 13, sc in second ch from hook and in each ch across (12 sc). Work 3 more sc in last ch. You will have 4 sc in end ch. Cont up other side, sc in each rem ch, 3 more sc in ch just worked (last st). Sl st in first sc — 30 sc. Mark rnds.

Rnd 2: Ch 2 (counts as hdc), hdc in each sc around, increasing 4 hdc on each end, to keep work flat — 38 hdc.

Rnd 3: Ch 2, hdc in each hdc around, inc 5 hdc on each end — 48 hdc.

Rnds 4-5: Ch 2, work even — 48 hdc around.

Rnd 6: Ch 2, work 4 inc evenly spaced around — 52 hdc.

Rnds 7-19: Rep Rnd 6. You should have 104 hdc on Rnd 19.

Rnd 20: Ch 2, work even with no inc. End off — 104 hdc.

Optional Lining: Cut stabilizer according to diagram. Cut lining fabric same as stabilizer, but cut ½" more on all outside edges. Attach lining to stabilizer (folding ½" extra fabric to other side) with fusible tape or fabric glue. Place bottom piece inside bottom of purse. Place both sides to inside of purse, overlapping each end. With sewing needle and thread, sew lining to purse with whip st while also sewing edges of lining tog on inside to fit.

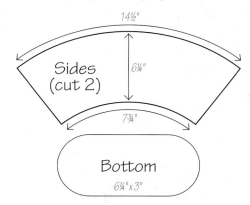

Sides (cut 2) — 14½" · 6¼" · 7¾"

Bottom — 6¼" x 3"

Finishing
For lp closure, attach yarn at center back st of purse. Ch 16, and sl st to same st as joining to form a lp. Sew button to center front of purse, approx. 1¼" down from top edge on center front of purse. With yarn and yarn needle, sew handles to front and back of purse, evenly spaced. Tuck sides of purse in about ½" at widest point, and st folded ends tog to secure. Weave in ends.

Materials:

2 skeins (100 g/80 yd. each) sari silk yarn or any other #5 yarn

Size H/8 (5 mm) hook

2 rattan and wood handles

1 wooden ¾" toggle button

Yarn needle

Sewing needle and matching thread

⅓ yd. fabric for lining (optional)

⅓ yd. ultra-firm stabilizer (optional)

Used in this project: Peltex #70 Ultra-Firm Stabilizer.

Gauge:
10 hdc = 3"

7 hdc rnds = 3"

To increase: work 2hdc in 1 st as indicated.

Words of Encouragement
Sometimes life can be challenging, and we all have inconsistencies or faults. With patience, your life can turn around, and you can become the beautiful person you were meant to be. I have found that life is a learning experience. It's not what life gives you, but what YOU give to life that makes the difference. Attitude is the key to everything! Just don't ever give up — God believes in you, but you have to believe in yourself.

Fits all sizes, depending on number of rows worked

BULKY
5
BULKY
Abultado

Sari Silk Hip Belt

Crochet this unique hip belt to go with your sari silk purse. A fun trim makes the belt even more special — wear with jeans or a skirt for an exotic, Bohemian look.

INSTRUCTIONS:

Row 1: Ch 8, sc in second ch from hook and in each ch across, ch 1, turn — 7 sc.

Rows 2-117 (or desired length): Sc in each sc across, ch 1, turn. End off after last row.

Bottom Edge

Attach yarn to one corner, working on long side, * ch 11, sk 6 rows, sl st to one lp only at next row; rep from * across row. End off — 17 ch-11 lps.

Closure

Work scs around entire metal half circle. End off. Attach half circle with yarn needle to one short end of belt. Attach button to other end on RS.

Top Edge

Attach yarn to any end st at top edge of belt, sc in end of second row and in end of each row across. Sk 3 rows, evenly spaced across to within last row, sl st to top of last row. End off — 112 sc + sl st at each end (3 dec made).

Finishing

With sewing needle and thread, attach beads to center of each ch-11 lp. Weave in ends.

Optional: Add fringe between ch-11 lps if desired.

Materials:

1 skein (100 g/80 yd.) sari silk yarn

Size E/4 (3.5 mm) hook

1 metal 1¼" half circle

1 wooden toggle button, 1½"-wide

17 metal beads

Yarn needle

Sewing needle and matching thread

Gauge:

7 sc = 2"

4 sc rows = 1⅛"

Helpful Hint:
If you start a project before you are finished with another one, make sure you attach a note to the first project listing the hook size you used. It will save you time and frustration.

Words of Encouragement

Believe in yourself and others will start believing in you. No matter what you are trying to accomplish in your life, don't let others who are more experienced intimidate you. If you need experience, just hang in there, taking one day at a time. Don't give up!

Skill Level — Beginner

FINE
2
FIN
Fino

Finished size — 7½", without toggle piece

Bracelet Watch

This chic watchband is one of the easiest crochet projects you'll
ever make. You can finish it in about an hour!

INSTRUCTIONS:

Sc circle — make 6 (more or less, depending on wrist size).

Loosely ch 2, in second ch work 15 sc, join to first sc. End off.

Note: Ch 2 loosely so the hole in the circle is big enough for the bead to fit. Then, the hole can be loosened or tightened with tail, depending on the bead size.

To Assemble:

Connect 1 circle to bar on each side of watch face with yarn needle and cord. If cord is too thick, you can untwist the cord and use 1 ply as your thread. Attach 2 more circles on each side (3 circles on each side total). With needle and thread, sew beads to inside of each circle. Sew toggle closure to each end.

Use black yarn for sophisticated elegance.

Materials:

1 spool (200 g/97 yd.) 100% nylon cord (see resources, pg. 125) in multi-color greens and dark red

Size D/3 (3.25 mm) hook

1 watch face with bars on sides (1"-1.4" in diameter)

1 silver toggle set for closure

6 flat ⅜" silver decorative beads

Yarn needle

Used in this project: Hilos 100% nylon cord #18 in color # 74, multi color-greens and cranberry (note: lighter green is cut off so circles will have only olive green and cranberry). Substitute J&P Coats Crochet nylon cord.

Gauge:

1 sc circle = 1" in diameter

Words of Encouragement

Do you just ride along and let life lead you to who knows where? Do you have a purpose or direction in your life? Terry, in his seminar, points out that if we haven't decided where we're going, we don't know which way to turn, and have no idea if we're off course. Having a clear idea of where you want to go reverses both of these problems. You have the power to control your destiny, so take control and find a purpose for living!

Misses sizes xs (sm, med, lg, xlg, 1x, 2x, 3x). All sizes from neck edge — approx. 19½" long

Ivory Shells Sweater

I was inspired to create the scalloped edging on this sweater by the design of a valance hanging in my living room. Creating your own unique designs can be fun and easy if you just keep your eyes open and think "outside the box." I had no idea that I'd get a crocheted sweater idea from my home decor!

INSTRUCTIONS:

Back

With G hook, loosely ch 68 (74, 80, 86, 92, 104, 110, 116).

Row 1: Sc in second ch from hook and in each ch across, ch 1, turn — 67 (73, 79, 85, 91, 103, 109, 115) sc.

This row should measure approx. 16½" (17½", 18½", 19½", 20½", 22½", 23½", 24½"). If this row is not the correct length, change your crochet hook until you achieve the correct gauge.

Row 2: * 1 sc in next sc, sk 2 sc, in next sc work (dc, ch 1, dc, ch 1, dc) for sh, sk 2 sc, rep from * across. End with 1 sc in last st, ch 4, turn — 11 (12, 13, 14, 15, 17, 18, 19) shs.

Row 3: (RS) 1 dc in first sc, * 1 sc in center dc of next sh, 1 sh in next sc, rep from * across, end with (1 dc, ch 1, and 1 dc) in last sc, ch 1, turn.

Row 4: 1 sc in first dc, * 1 sh in next sc, 1 sc in center dc of next sh, rep from * across. End with 1 sc in tch, ch 4, turn.

Rep Rows 3 and 4 in patt, until piece measures approx. 16"-16¼" from beg (all sizes). End with row 3.

Front

Work same as back. With RS tog, sew side seams with yarn and yarn needle

Armhole Opening

Turn RS out.

Pm to st next to side seam at left, and another marker to st at rt of side seam. Attach yarn to st where marker was placed at rt of seam, ch 42 (48, 54, 60, 66, 78, 84, 90). Being careful not to twist ch, attach with sl st to st at left of seam, where marker was placed. End off. Rep on other side. Without stretching ch, lp should measure 4½" (5", 5½", 6", 6½", 7½", 8", 8½") when folded.

Yoke

Worked in rnds — pm at beg of each rnd. You will be working across front, armhole ch, back and armhole ch.

Row 1: Attach yarn to same sp as sl st, where marker was placed at left of seam. Ch 4, dc in same st, ch 1, dc (sh made), * sc in top of center dc of sh, sh in next sc, rep from * across front to next armhole ch, sh in same sp where marker was placed [beg ch of ch 42 (48, 54, 60, 66, 78, 84, 90)], * Sk 2 chs, sc in next ch, sk 2 chs, sh in next ch, rep from last * around, skipping last 2 chs of armhole chs, work sh in same sp as joining where marker was placed to left of seam — 8 (9, 10, 11, 12, 14, 15, 16) shs across armhole ch (which includes 1 sh at each corner), sc in top of next sh, cont in patt around. When you get to second armhole ch, work sh in sp as first joining and cont around. End with sk last 2 chs of armhole ch, join to ch 3 of first dc (first sh made) 6 (7, 8, 9, 10, 12, 13, 14) shs across each armhole ch + extra sh at each sp where marker was — 36 (38, 40, 42, 44, 48, 50, 52) shs.

Rnd 2: Sl st to center dc of next sh, sc in same sp, sh in next sc, cont in patt around, end with sl st in first sc — 36 (38, 40, 42, 44, 48, 50, 52) shs.

Rnd 3 (dec rnd): Pm at each st directly above where markers were placed at each end of armhole ch, ch 4 (counts as dc + ch 1) sc in top of next sh, work in patt around, working

Materials:

14 (15, 16, 17, 18, 20, 21) hanks (1.75 oz./ 50 g/100 yd. each) 59% rayon, 41% wool yarn in ivory

Size G/6 (4 mm) and H/8 (5 mm) hooks

Used in this project: Berroco Softwist in Vanilla. Caron Simply Soft or Red Heart Soft Yarn are great substitutes, but you will have to use a much larger hook (like a size K) to get the correct gauge.

Gauge:

3 shells (2 sc between) = 4"

5 shell rows = 2½"

4 dc on collar = 1"

Gauge is very important with this sweater. If your gauge does not match, change to a different-size hook.

Special Stitch:

Shell (sh): On body of sweater (dc, ch 1, dc, ch 1, dc) in same st.

Popcorn Stitch (pc): Ch 4, work 4 more dc in same st, take yarn off hook, slip hook through third ch of beg ch-4, placing hook behind 5 dc, put loose lp back onto hook, pull through ch 3 of ch-4 (in back) ch 1 loosely from front, sl st through same sp at base of pc st.

To Decrease Shell: Work 1 dc in sp (sc that is marked) instead of 3 dc shell.

Words of Encouragement

Many of us love trendy things and keep up with the latest styles. A young lady needs to be aware that drawing attention doesn't necessarily mean that she looks sharp. Clothing that is revealing or just plain weird may draw attention, but most people will perceive this as a girl trying to compensate for feelings of inadequacy. Be mindful of the trends you choose to follow and who you may be influencing.

1 dc (dec) in each marked st instead of a 3-dc sh. End with sc in top of last sh and sl st to ch 3 of ch 4 — 32 (34, 36, 38, 40, 44, 46, 48) shs + 1 dc in each marked sp (4 decs on rnd).

Rnd 4: Pm at 4 sps on Rnd 3, evenly spaced (2 on front and 2 on back). Ch 4, (dc, ch 1, dc) in same sp (sh made). Cont in patt around, working sh in each sp where dcs were placed on prev rnd (at beg and end of armhole), and work 1 dc where markers were placed, join, 28 (30, 32, 34, 36, 40, 42, 44) shs — 4 decs.

Rnd 5: Sh in same sp (ch 4, dc, ch 1, dc) pm in center front sc. Rep on back, cont around in patt, working 1 dc in same sp as marker, and sh in same sp as dc, join — 26 (28, 30, 32, 34, 38, 40, 42) shs — 2 decs.

Rnds 6 and 7: Work in patt, with no decs — 26 (28, 30, 32, 34, 38, 40, 42) shs.

Rnd 8: Mark center sc on each armhole; work in patt around, dec in sps at markers, join — 24 (26, 28, 30, 32, 36, 38, 40) shs — 2 decs.

Rnd 9: Mark 1 sc on front and 1 sc on back, in a different sp as before; work in patt around — 22 (24, 26, 28, 30, 34, 36, 38) shs — 2 decs.

Rnd 10: Rep Rnd 9. End off — 20 (22, 24, 26, 28, 32, 34, 36) shs — 2 decs.

Sleeves
Rnd 1: Working in loose lps on opp side of ch at armhole ch, attach yarn to sp at base of any sh, ch 1, sc in same sp, sk 2 chs, sh in base of next sc, sk 2 chs, sc in base of next sh, cont working in patt until you have 8 (9, 10, 11, 12, 14, 15, 16) shs. End with sl st in first sc.

Rnd 2: (Ch 4, dc, ch 1, dc) in same sp, sc in top of next sh, work in patt around. End with sc in top of last sh and sl st to ch 3 of ch 4 — 8 (9, 10, 11, 12, 14, 15, 16) shs.

Rnd 3: Sl st over to middle dc of sh, ch 1, sc in same sp, work in patt around, end with sl st in first sc.

Rnds 4-30: Rep Rows 2 and 3 or until sleeves measure approx. 15" (or desired length) from beg of first rnd. End off. If you want sleeve to narrow a little to wrist (before flare is added), start crocheting a more tightly from Rnd 24 to end.

Rep Rnds 1-30 for other sleeve.

Flare on End of Sleeve

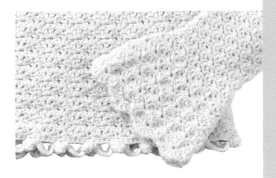

Attach yarn to any sc on last rnd worked, to sc that is at fold (on side closest to side of sweater) when lying flat.

Rnd 1: (If you crocheted tighter on bottom of sleeve, start working sts normally here.) Ch 4 (counts as dc + ch 1) dc, ch 1, dc, ch 1, dc (4 dc sh made) in same sc as sl st. Cont in patt around — 8 (9, 10, 11, 12, 14, 15, 16) shs.

Rnds 2-3: Cont in patt, working a 4-dc sh in each sc between shs.

Rnds 4-7: Work 5 dc shs around.

Rnds 8-10: Work 6 dc shs around. End off.

Collar
All dcs in blo — collar should measure 5¼"-5½" vertically.

Attach yarn to any sc on neck edge, ch 1, sc in same sp, and in each st around, join to first sc. End off. If neck edge is too loose, sk some scs on this rnd by doing the following: Decide how many sts you want to dec, and pm in that number of scs evenly spaced around. While working scs around, as in step 1, sk scs where markers were placed. End off.

Row 1: Change to size H hook. Work collar with loose dcs.

Attach yarn to any sc on inside/WS of neck edge, ch 21. Dc in fourth ch from hook and in each ch across (19 dc — all sizes) sk next sc, tightly sl st in next 2 sc, ch 1, turn.

Row 2: Dc in blo of each dc across; end with dc in tch, ch 3 (counts as first dc from here on out), turn — 19 dc.

Row 3: Sk first dc, dc in blo of next 18 dc, sk next sc, tightly sl st in next 2 sc, ch 1, turn — 19 dc total.

Rep Rows 2 and 3 around entire neck edge. End off. With RS tog, sew first row to last row with yarn needle.

Scalloped Edge — Bottom of Sweater
Row 1: Change to size G hook. Starting on WS (inside edge) of sweater, attach yarn to st that is to left of side seam (directly above st where sh is on Row 1). * Ch 9, sk 5 sts, sl st in next st, and rep from * around entire bottom edge.

Note: When you get to next side seam, sl st again over seam and into st directly above sh on row 1. Cont around; end with sl st to st that is to rt of st where yarn was attached at beg. Ch 1, turn. (You'll be working above same sts as sc and sh on Row 1 of front and back — sl sts and popcorns on next row go here.)

Row 2: (Popcorn st row) Front side — * In ch-9 lp, work 9 sc. Ch 1, sl st to same sp as sl st before next ch 9 (between ch 9s). In same sp work pc st (see special sts) ch 1, rep from * around, end with pc between last and first ch-9 lp. End off.

Edging for Collar- Front Facing

Rnd 1: With H hook and being careful not to pull too tight, attach yarn on bottom edge of collar at seam, ch 1, sc in same sp, sc in side of dc, sc in st between first and second row. Cont working scs around entire collar edge, making sure you work a sc in side of each dc and a sc in sp between each row, sl st to first sc, turn.

Rnd 2: Change to G hook. Sl st to first sc that is to left of seam, * ch 12, sk 7 sc, sl st in next sc, rep from * around, end with sl st in first sc, ch 4, turn.

Note: If you end up with extra rows on your collar, you'll have to adjust the number of sts between ch 12s and you may have to ch more or less than 12 to get it to hang right. This is general instruction — each person may have a different number of st on their rnd in step 1 of collar.

Rnd 3: * Pc in same st, ch 1, in ch 12 work (12 sc, ch 1), sl st in next st (between ch 12 lps), rep from * around. End with sl st in st before first pc. End off.

Finishing
If you have holes or spaces where you attached the yarn to start working the sleeves at the armholes, this is because your beg ch across the arm is too loose. To fix the problem, just untwist 1 ply from yarn and carefully sew hole (from the WS) with a sewing needle. Weave in ends.

Helpful Hint:
Remember that crocheting is incredibly easy! All it takes is a little patience to learn how to hold the hook and yarn. If you stick with it, you can make almost anything!

Skill Level — Advanced Beginner

SUPER FINE

1

SUPER FIN
Super Fino

Finished size — 14" x 1⅜", one size fits most (adjustable)

Lacy Choker

This dainty little choker is a great "rainy day" project. It works up in two hours or less, even if you are not used to working with small thread. Replace the pearls with sparkly crystals that will brighten every day.

INSTRUCTIONS

Row 1: Ch 109, dc in sixth ch from hook, * ch 1, sk 1 ch, dc in next st, rep from * across, turn — 54 dc and 53 ch-1 sps.

Row 2: * Ch 7, sk 1 dc, sc in next dc, rep from * across, turn — 26 lps.

Row 3: Sl st to lp, ch 1, 3 sc in ch-7 lp, * ch 5, 3 sc in next lp, rep from * across, ch 1, turn — 25 lps.

Row 4: Sl st to center of lp, ** ch 5, dc in next ch-5 lp, * ch 5, sl st in fifth ch from hook for p. Rep from * twice, dc in top of last dc, dc in same sp with last dc, ch 5, sc in next lp, rep from ** across. End with sc in last lp. End off, and weave in ends.

Finishing

Sew button to one end of choker. Use a ch-5 or ch-7 at other end for buttonhole.

Optional: Sew pearls or beads to center of each three-leaf clover with needle and thread.

Materials:

1 ball (400 yd.) #10 100% mercerized crochet cotton thread in rose

US size 8 (1.25 mm) steel hook

½" ivory button

13 small pearls or beads

Sewing needle and thread to match

Used in this project: Aunt Lydia's Classic Crochet Cotton in Dusty Rose. Substitute J and P Coats Knit Cro Sheen in Almond Pink.

Gauge:

4 dcs with ch in between each dcs = 1"

Ch 5 = ½"

Three-leaf clover = ⅝"

Special Stitch:

Three-Leaf Clover (clo): Ch 5, sl st in fifth ch from hook (3 times).

Picot (p): Ch 5, sl st in fifth ch from hook.

Words of Encouragement

Do you hate rainy days or do you love them? I used to get really annoyed when it rained because everything was so wet and gloomy, but over the years I have come to love and appreciate a rainy day. It's downright cozy, and I just love to hear rain falling on a tin roof. My husband tells people that if God said to him, "You only have one day left to live, but it will be raining," he would say to God, "I'll take it!" That could change the way you look at any day, no matter what the weather.

Finished size — 72"

Skill Level — Advanced Beginner

MEDIUM
4
MOYEN
Medio

Framed Flower Scarf

Brighten up someone's day with a lovely gift. This fresh, flowery scarf is just the thing to put a smile on anyone's face, and they will never forget how wonderful you made them feel!

Crochet a whole garden of different framed flowers!

Materials:

1 skein each (5 oz./140 g/
256 yd.) soft yarn in
dark purple (A) and bright
green (B)

Size G/6 (4 mm) hook

Yarn needle

*Used in this project: Red
Heart Soft Yarn in Grape
and Guacamole*

Gauge:

1 square = 4"

1 6-petal flower = 4¼"

7 sc (square) = 1⅝"

2 dc (flower) = ½"

INSTRUCTIONS:
Framed Flower Square
Make 17.

Rnd 1: With color A, ch 4, sl st in first ch to form ring, ch 1, 8 sc into ring, sl st in first sc.

Rnd 2: * Loosely ch 6, sl st in second ch from hook, sc in next ch, hdc in next ch, sc in next 2 chs, sl st in next sc on ring, rep from * 7 more times. End off — 8 petals.

Rnd 3: Attach color B in top of any pet, ch 5, dc in same sp, *ch 4, sl st in top of next pet, ch 4, (dc, ch 2, dc) in top of next pet, rep from * around. End with sl st in third ch of ch-5.

Rnd 4: Sl st to center of ch 2, ch 1, * (3 sc, ch 2, 3 sc) in corner ch-2 sp, 4 sc in ch-4 sp, sk sl st, 4 sc in next ch-4 sp. Rep from * 3 times, sl st in first sc.

Rnd 5: Ch 1, sc in joining st and in next 2 sc, * 3 sc in corner ch-2 sp, sc in each of next 14 sc to next corner. Rep from * around, sl st to first sc made. End off.

Finishing
Weave in all loose ends. Sew squares tog with yarn and yarn needle.

Picot Edge
Attach A to center edge. * Ch 3, sl st in first ch (p made), sk 2 sts, sl st to next st, rep from * around entire edge of scarf, skipping only 1 st at each of 4 corners.

Helpful Hint:

If you are not in a crochet group, why not start one in your home? Invite everyone you know who crochets, and tell them to bring friends. Make it fun by having crochet-related games and door prizes like yarn, hooks, pattern books, hook cases, tote bags for carrying yarn or gauge wizards. I try to make sure everyone gets a prize. If you are a beginner, being part of a crochet group will help you learn.

Words of Encouragement
When you give a gift from the heart, that act of kindness may mean more than you ever realize. I read once, "People won't necessarily remember what you say, and they won't always remember what you do, but they will always remember the way you made them feel." How do you make the important people in your life feel? Do you discourage them or lift them up?

Skill Level — Beginner

MEDIUM
4
MOYEN
Medio

Size before felting — 11½" tall and 16½" wide, when flat , size after felting — 10½" tall x 11½" wide, without straps

Chocolate Felted Tote

The agitation of your washing machine puts the finishing touch on this thick and sturdy tote, roomy enough to carry your yarn project or any other larger items. It could even be a fashionable diaper bag! An optional pocket on one side carries your cell phone, keys or sunglasses.

INSTRUCTIONS:

Tote Bottom

Tote is made using 2 strands of yarn.

Row 1: With 2 strands of yarn ch 37, hdc in third ch from hook, and in each ch across, turn — 36 hdc.

Row 2: Ch 2 (counts as beg hdc), hdc in each hdc across, turn — 36 hdc.

Rows 3-7: Rep Row 2, turning after each row. Do not end off after row 7, but cont with Rnd 1 of tote body. Bottom should measure approx. 15" x 4¾" before felting.

Body of Tote

Rnd 1: Ch 2 (counts as first hdc), 2 hdc in first hdc, hdc around entire bottom rectangle piece, working 3 hdc in each corner and 9 hdc evenly spaced along short sides. Join with sl st to ch 2. Do not turn — 98 hdc.

Rnd 2: Ch 2, hdc in each hdc around. Join to tch — 98 hdc.

Rnds 3–27: Rep Rnd 2 or for 11½". End off.

Tote will measure approx. 16½" wide.

Straps

Make 2. With 2 strands, loosely ch 105.

Row 1: Hdc in third ch from hook and in each ch across, ch 1, turn — 104 dc.

Row 2: Sc in each hdc across. End off. Fold strap and loosely sew long edges tog with yarn and yarn needle, forming a long tube. End off. Straps will be sewn on after felting.

Pocket

With 2 strands, ch 21.

Row 1: Hdc in third ch from hook and in each ch across, ch 2, turn — 20 hdc.

Row 2: Hdc in each hdc across, ch 2, turn — 20 hdc.

Rows 3-12: Rep Row 2, omitting ch 2 after Row 12. Pocket should measure 5½" x 7¼". Sew pocket to side of tote with yarn and yarn needle before felting. Weave in ends.

To felt, see pg 9. After last spin cycle, place tote on box covered with plastic bag that fits tightly to hold its shape. Dry completely. Straighten straps by stretching before drying.

Finishing

Pin trim onto tote ½" from top edge. Sew in place with needle and thread. Pm where you want straps, and sew to inside of tote.

Optional lining: Cut piece of interfacing 23" x 10¾" (½" smaller than width of tote). This will be one long piece that will fit front, back and bottom of tote, omitting sides. Cut piece of fabric 1" longer than interfacing to fold over short ends, and 2½" wider than long sides of interfacing. See Diagram A.

Diagram A — Fabric wrong side / Fold / Stabilizer / Fold over 1" / 2½"

Fold 1" of fabric over short ends and sew or glue tog. Do not fold sides of fabric over stabilizer. Sew or glue fabric and stabilizer tog on long sides, leaving 2½" of fabric on sides. Fold piece in half and sew up sides on outer edges with ½" seam, leaving short ends open and making sure RS of fabric shows inside tote. Place piece inside tote and adjust to fit if necessary. Hand st lining to inside of purse.

Materials:

- 4 skeins (3.5 oz./100 g/ 223 yd. each) 100% wool worsted-wt. yarn in chestnut brown
- Size J/10 (6 mm) hook
- 33" beaded trim
- 1 large snap
- Yarn needle
- Sewing needle and matching thread
- ½ yd. fabric for lining (optional)
- 23" x 10¾" stabilizer

Used in this project: Patons Classic Merino Wool in Chestnut Brown, Peltex.

Note: If you use one strand to make the tote, you will only need two skeins of yarn, but the tote will be smaller.

Gauge:

8 hdc and 6 rows = 3"

Special trims make your purse stand out.

Words of Encouragement

Are you and your mate often agitated with each other? It's not a fun way to live. I have friends who used to fight day and night, but today they get along great. I had to ask my friend their secret. She said, "You want to really know what made us stop fighting? We just got sick and tired of fighting!" It was one of the best decisions they ever made.

Skill Level — Beginner

BULKY
5
BULKY
Abultado

Finished size — one size fits most

Oversized Hat

This hat can be worn two ways. Wear it as a snood (a person with dreadlocks will look great!), or roll up the edges for a totally different look. This hat coordinates with the Patchwork Purse.

INSTRUCTIONS:

Hat

With color A, ch 31 to measure 12¼".

Row 1: Sc in second ch from hook and in each ch across, ch 1, turn — 30 sc.

Rows 2-4: Sc in blo of each sc across, ch 1 turn. After row 4, end off, turn. Attach B to blo of first sc. After every fourth row, attach next color and cont working in patt with each sc in blo with 4 sc rows per color — 30 sts per row.

Work in patt until you have 60 rows. End off. With RS tog, sew last row to first row, forming a tube. End off. Turn hat RS out.

Top

Pm at first sc at beg of every rnd.

Rnd 1: Attach yarn with sl st to ridge, at end of any row on one open end of hat, sc in same sp. Sc in every ridge around, sl st to first sc — 31 sc (includes 30 ridges + seam = 31).

Rnd 2: Ch 1, starting with first sc, * draw up a lp in each of next 2 sc, yo, draw through all 3 lps on hook (1 st dec). Rep from * 14 more times, sl st to first sc, sc in last sc — 16 sc.

Rnd 3: Ch 1, * draw up a lp in each of next 3 sc, yo, draw through all 4 lps on hook, and rep from * until hole is closed. End off.

Border

Rnd 1: Working along other edge of hat, work 1 sc at end of each row around, sl st to first sc — 60 sc.

Rnd 2: Ch 1, * sc in next sc, 2sctog (dec) in next 2 sc, rep from * around, sl st to first sc — 40 sc.

Rnd 3: Ch 1, sc in each sc around, sl st to first sc. End off.

Wear the hat as a snood if you have dreadlocks.

Materials:

- 1 skein (3 oz./85 g/ 135 yd.) each bulky yarn in fuchsia (A), plum (B), blue (C) and green (D)
- Size K/10.5 (6.5 mm) hook
- Yarn needle

Used in this project: Lion Brand Jiffy yarn in Fuchsia (A) Plum (B) Peacock (C) and Grass Green (D).

Gauge:

- 4 sc = 1½"
- 4 sc rows = 1¾" (without stretching)

Words of Encouragement

Do people "dread" to be around you? Are you pleasant or always grouchy? You are capable of changing the circumstances in your family environment by controlling your speech and emotions. Change sometimes seems hard, but "with God all things are possible"! All you have to do is decide and act on it.

Helpful Hint:
For a hat that is less full, work fewer rows.

Skill Level — Beginner

Finished size — 11" x 11" (without strap)

Patchwork Purse

This colorful shoulder bag is very easy to make, and it has an interesting texture. The simple single crochet stitch was used to form the ridges. The pretty decorative button sets it off perfectly!

INSTRUCTIONS:

Square

Make 6 squares each of A, B, C and MC, and 8 squares in D — 32 total.

Row 1: Ch 11, sc in second ch from hook and in each ch across, ch 1, turn — 10 sc.

Rows 2-9: Sc in blo of each sc, ch 1, turn — 10 sc. At end of Row 9, end off.

To Assemble

Place squares on flat surface in any color order using photo as a guide. Be sure to alternate the direction of the ridges on the squares as you lay them out. With RS tog, sew squares tog with yarn and yarn needle (16 squares for front and 16 squares for back). With RS tog, sew front to back at sides and across bottom. If you are making a lining, you do not need to weave in the loose ends.

Top Edge

Attach MC to top edge of purse at side seam, ch 1, sc in each st and sp around top. End off.

Strap

Row 1: On either side seam, attach green yarn to st that is to RS of seam. Tightly ch 100, sl st to other side of purse to st at RS of seam, sl st to next sc to left of seam, ch 1, turn.

Row 2: Sc in each sc across, sl st to next 2 sc on top edge of purse, ch 1, turn — 100 sc.

Row 3: Sc across row, sl st to next sc on top edge. End off.

Row 4: Join yarn in st on opp side (loose ls) of beg ch, sc in each lp across. End off.

Tassels

Make 2 tassels, 6" each.

Wrap yarn around 6" piece of cardboard 15 times. Slip a 12" piece of yarn under the yarn at top of cardboard and tie tight knot, leaving ends to attach tassel to purse. Remove from cardboard. Cut another 12" piece of yarn, wrap around top of tassel about ½" from the top, and tie knot. Trim ends evenly.

With yarn needle, weave remaining loose ends into center of tassel. Attach 1 tassel to each bottom corner of purse.

Materials:

- 1 ball (3 oz./85 g) each yarn in fuchsia (A), plum (B), blue (C), taupe (D) and green (MC)
- Size I/9 (5.5 mm) hook
- 1" decorative button
- ½ yd. fabric for lining (optional)
- Yarn needle
- 6" piece of cardboard
- Sewing needle and matching thread for lining

Used in this project: Lion Brand Jiffy yarn in Peacock, Plum, Fuchsia, Grass Green (MC), and Taupe (D).

Gauge:

- 1 square = 3" x 3"
- 10 sc = 3"
- 9 sc rows = 3"

Words of Encouragement

Have you come to ridges, bumps or roadblocks along your path? Obstacles are not fun, and they can really slow us down. Maybe these things come along and slow us down to help build patience. Instead of getting frustrated, ask "what can I learn here?" The bumps and ridges in life can strengthen us. Just get back up when you fall down!

Optional Lining: Cut fabric 25½" x 13½". With RS tog, fold fabric in half (fold will be at bottom of purse). Sew side seams with a ¾" seam, leaving top open. Place lining inside purse (WS tog), adjusting if necessary. Fold top lining edge under ¾". Pin top edge of lining to inside of bag. Whip st lining to bag with needle and thread.

Closure

Sew button to purse front with needle and thread. For button lp, attach yarn to top edge of back at center st. Ch 38, join to same st where ch was started. End off.

Try using other colors to match different outfits.

Skill Level — Advanced Beginner

MEDIUM
4
MOYEN
Medio

Finished size — 83" x 6¼"

Cloverleaf Scarf

I love designing three-dimensional projects or anything that dangles. The three-leaf clovers are part of what make this scarf unique, and even though it's easy, the beginning chain is extra-long. The beginning chain is the most difficult part of the whole pattern, but it is so pretty when it is finished!

45

Materials:

1 skein (7 oz./225 g/
335 yd.) yarn in burgundy

Size H/8 (5 mm) hook

Yarn needle

Used in this project:
Bernat Super Value
in Burgundy

Gauge:

1 Three-Leaf Clover = 1⅞"

8 dc = 3"

4 dc rows = 2⅞"

Special Stitch:

Three-Leaf Clover (clo):
Ch 7, sl st in seventh ch
from hook, 3 times.

INSTRUCTIONS:

Row 1: Ch 222, dc in fourth ch from hook, and in each ch across, ch 3, turn — 220 dc.

Rows 2-4: Sk first dc, dc in each dc across, ch 3, turn, do not ch 3 at end of fourth row. End off. Turn scarf to front side, attach yarn to rt corner st on short end. Working first sc in same st as joining, and 2 sc in middle, work 11 sc total across short end. End off. Rep on other end — 11 sc on each end.

Three-Leaf Clo St Edging Rnd Attach yarn to first st at rt corner of long side on front, * Ch 4, (ch 7, sl st in seventh ch from hook) 3 times — 3 leaf clo st made, 1 sl st in ch before first leaf, ch 4, sk 3 dc, sl st in next st, rep from * around entire scarf, working up both sides. End off — 114 three-leaf clos.

Note: Work 2 three-leaf dangling clover sets on each end.

Work Clovers in Center

Fold scarf in half with RS showing. Pm to center st at fold. Count down 5 sts (dcs) Place another marker in center. Count down 6 sts. Pm. Cont down side of scarf toward end, placing marker after every 6 sts, rep on other side of fold — 37 markers.

Clovers

Start at center working toward end, then work clos going in opp direction on other end, so they will lay right when scarf is placed around neck. Attach yarn around st where marker was placed, work a 3 leaf clo, sl st in same sp where yarn was attached. End off, rep at each marker — 37 three-leaf clos.

Helpful Hint:

If one side of your scarf is tighter than the other, weave in a piece of yarn on the loose side and pull to make them even.

Words of Encouragement

The beginning of anything is usually the most difficult phase. If you are beginning a marriage and are discouraged because it's harder than you expected, remember that you've never been a spouse before. You have to practice, just as in anything, to increase your skill. Working on your inner qualities will help to make the transition easier.

Finished size — 10" tall x 10¾" wide (without handles)

Double-Breasted Jacket Purse

This unique purse will certainly attract attention. As you proudly carry it, nobody will know that you made it yourself. Be careful, though — if they do find out, you'll probably get more orders than you can handle!

Materials:

2 rolls (7 oz./200 g each) nylon cord in hot pink

Size F/5 (3.75 mm) hook

1 ball (1.75 oz./55 yd.) black fur yarn

4 large black buttons, 1½" in diameter

2 decorative purse handles with silver and black beads

Yarn needle

⅓ yd. fabric for lining (optional)

⅓ yd. extra-firm stabilizer (optional)

Sewing needle and matching thread

Used in this project: Hilos # 18 100% nylon cord in Hot Pink (see resources, pg. 125), Lion Brand Festive Fur in black, Peltex extra-firm stabilizer. Substitute J&P Coats Crochet Nylon Cord.

Gauge:

6 pattern sts (sc and dc alternating sts) = 1½"

8 rows = 2"

Stitch Pattern: alternating sc and dc

Helpful Hint

Nylon cord can be slippery, making it hard to weave in ends. Try using a fabric glue, such as "OK To Wash It", to secure ends to the purse after they are woven through.

INSTRUCTIONS:

Bottom

Rnd 1: Ch 29, 4 sc in second ch from hook, sc in next 26 chs, 4 sc in last ch. Working along opp side of starting ch, sc in next 26 chs, sl st to first sc — 60 sc.

Rnd 2: Ch 1, 2 sc in same sp as joining, 2 sc in each of next 4 sc, sc in each of next 25 sc to end, 2 sc in each of 5 sc on curved end, sc in each of next 25 sc, sl st to first sc — 70 sc (10 incs).

Rnd 3: Ch 1, * 2 sc in next sc, sc in next sc, rep from * 4 more times, sc in next 25 sc, (2 sc in next sc, 1 sc in next sc) 5 times, sc in next 25 sc, sl st to first sc — 80 sc.

Rnd 4: Ch 1, sc in each sc around, join — 80 sc.

Rnd 5: Ch 1,* (sc in next 2 sc, 2 sc in next sc, sc in next 2 sc) 3 times, sc in next 25 sc; rep from * and join with sl st — 86 sc.

Rnd 6: Work sc in each sc around, in(cing) 2 sc on each end, join — 90 sc.

Rnd 7: Ch 1, working sc in each sc around, inc 3 sc on each end, join — 96 sc.

Rnd 8: Ch 1, sc in each sc around with no inc — 96 sc.

Rnd 9: Ch 1, sc in each sc around, working 4 incs on each end, join. End off — 104 sc.

Trace bottom of purse onto cardboard to use later as pattern for stabilizer and lining bottom (should measure approx. 10" x 3¾").

Body of Purse

This rectangle piece will be sewn to bottom and overlapped at front.

Row 1: Starting at top edge, ch 112, sc in second ch from hook, * dc in next ch, sc in next ch, rep from *. End with sc in last ch, turn — 111 sts.

Row 2: Ch 1, * dc in sc, sc in dc, rep from *. End with dc in sc, turn — 111 sts.

Row 3: Ch 1, * sc in next st, dc in next st, rep from *, end with sc in last st, ch 1, turn.

Row 4: Rep Row 2.

Row 5: Rep Row 3.

Cont in patt, alternating Rows 4 and 5 until piece measures 7½" from beg ch.

Next row: Mark beg of next row. At beg of this row, work 2ststog (1 dec made). Cont in patt, dec 1 st at marked edge, every other row (curving that edge in as shown in photo). Work until piece measures 9". End off (curved edge will be at bottom).

Work 1 row of scs around sides and bottom edge, leaving top edge of purse unworked. You may have to inc some sts on curved edge or dec some sts on short sides if necessary, so body of purse will lay flat. Do not work scs on top edge.

Attaching Body of Purse to Bottom Piece

Using photo as a guide, pin bottom of purse to sides, overlapping front curved edge to other end. Baste top to bottom with piece of yarn. Start attaching body of purse to bottom at

Words of Encouragement

Isn't it fun to receive a gift when someone is thoughtful enough to remember you? We all love gifts, receiving phone calls, cards and being invited over for lunch. Even though we should not expect anything in return, sometimes it doesn't seem to occur to people to return the favor and reach out. Be a giver as well as a receiver.

end that will be underneath flap, and sew bottom edge to purse bottom with a topstitch/whipstitch on outside edges using cord and yarn needle. Do not pull too tight. End off. Before attaching short side of purse tog, turn purse inside out and weave in loose ends. Sew flap that is to be over-lapped to purse through both pieces with needle and thread from inside, leaving edge a little loose.

Optional Lining: Use cardboard tracing as a pattern to cut a piece of stabilizer for bottom of purse. Tack stabilizer to bottom of purse. For extra firmness, cut a piece of plastic canvas and glue to bottom stabilizer. Cut a rectangular piece of stabilizer to fit inside of purse. Tack stabilizer to sides of purse with needle and thread. Cut a purse bottom out of fabric using the cardboard as a pattern and adding a 1/3" seam allowance.

Cut a piece of lining fabric 10¼" high by 26" wide. Pin "side" lining to "bottom" lining. Place lining in purse and pin side seam. Sew bottom and side seam by hand or machine. Insert lining into purse, WS tog. Adjust length of lining by turning top edge to inside and pinning in place. Whip st top edge of lining to top edge of purse. (Be sure stitching does not interfere with sts on top edge of purse that will be used for trim.)

Top Edge
Attach fur yarn with F hook to any st at top edge of purse, sc in same st and in each st around. End off. If you want fur to be wider, rep rows of sc with fur for desired length.

Finishing
Weave in ends. Sew buttons to front of purse using photo as a guide. Sew handles to front and back at top edges.

Finished size — 51" x 6½"

SUPER FINE

1

SUPER FIN
Super Fino

MEDIUM

4

MOYEN
Medio

Purse Lover's Scarf

This cute scarf will surely be an attention grabber. Women of all
ages love purses, so make this scarf for a unique fashion statement.

INSTRUCTIONS:

Rose Purse

Row 1: With #5 hook and B, ch 20, sc in second ch from hook and in each ch, ch 1, turn — 19 sc.

Row 2: 1 dec in first 2 sc, sc in next 15 sc, 1 dec in last 2 sc, ch 1, turn — 17 sc.

Row 3: Work even with no decs, ch 1, turn — 17 sc.

Rows 4-7: Cont in patt, dec 1 sc on each end every other row. Row 7=13 sc. End off.

Trim

Approx. two-thirds down from top, weave C between rows with sewing needle.

With #8 steel hook and C, ch 29. Fold into bow and sew center to purse.

Handle

Sew 2 small rings to top edge of purse. Attach thread to 1 ring, ch 19, attach to other ring, ch 1, turn, sl st in each ch across, attach to ring. End off.

Striped Purse

Do not turn rows.

Row 1: For bottom, with # 5 hook and D, ch 12, sc in each sc across. End off — 11 sc.

Side Stripes - Front

Row 1: With C, ch 12, sc in second ch and rem chs. End off. Do not turn — 11 sc.

Row 2: Attach B to first sc, sc in each sc. End off.

Row 3: Rep Row 2 with D. Rep Rows 1-3 twice more. Work 11 rows total changing colors every row. Sew D piece to bottom. Make handle same as Rose Purse, using E hook and ch 15.

Green Purse

Row 1: With C and #5 hook, ch 10, sc in second ch from hook and in each ch across, ch 1, turn — 9 sc.

Row 2: Inc on each end — 11 sc.

Row 3: Work even with no incs — 11 sc.

Rows 4-9: Rep Rows 2 and 3. Row 9 should have 17 sc. End off.

Note: On Row 7, change to B, and in every other sc, work a long sc in st of row below. Change back to C on Row 8. Make handles same as Rose Purse, with 14 chs. End off.

Materials:

1 skein (7 oz./225 g/ 335 yd.) black yarn (A)

1 ball each (150 yd.) crochet cotton #3 in rose (B), green (C), yellow (D) and tan (E)

Size J/10 (6 mm) and C/2 (2.75 mm) hooks

US Steel hooks #5 (1.7 mm) and #8 (1.25 mm) for purses

6 tiny silver circles to make jewelry

1 tiny crystal or bead for purse closure

Yarn needle

Sewing needle and matching thread

Used in this project: Bernat Super Value yarn in black, J&P Coats Royale Fashion Crochet Thread #3 in Rose (B), green (C), yellow (D) and tan (E). To substitute #10 thread, double it throughout the pattern.

Gauge:

4 sts = 1½"

4 rows = 2"

2 sc on purses = ¼"

3 sc rows on purses = ⅓"

Words of Encouragement

Norman Vincent Peale said, "Anything you can conceive, and believe, you can achieve!" From the time they were small, our children were taught to believe they could accomplish anything they desired in life. Our youngest son used to go around making that statement when he was seven years old, and today he has his doctorate in marriage and family therapy. Our other son and daughter are equally as successful in life.

Scarf

Row 1: With A, and J hook, ch 16. Sc in second ch from hook and each ch across, ch 1, turn — 15 sc.

Row 2: * Sc in next sc, dc in next sc, rep from *. End with sc in last sc, ch 1, turn — 15 sts.

Row 3: * dc in next sc, sc in next dc, rep from *. End with dc in last sc, ch 1, turn — 15 sts.

Rows 4-116: Rep Rows 2 and 3. End off.

Pink Shell (sh) Edging

With size C hook and (B) attach to side edge of scarf rt before last 2 rows on long edge (space that's indented). Ch 1, sc in same sp, ** 9 dc in corner, * sk approx. ¾", sc, sk ¾", 7 dc. Rep from * twice, sk ¾", sc in next st, 9 dc in corner. You should have 3 7-dc shs across short end of scarf, and a 9-dc sh at each corner. Cont on other long edge of scarf, sk 2 rows, sc, * sk 2 rows, 7 dc sh, sk 2 rows, sc. Rep from * to within last 2 rows, sc before second to last row, rep from ** around rem edge, sl st in first sc. End off — 28 shs on each long edge, 66 shs total.

Fits sizes xs (sm, med, lg, xlg, 1x, 2x)

FINE
2
FIN
Fino

Cloverleaf Top

You're sure to get lots of compliments in this funky top with dangling cloverleaves. Wear it on a warm summer evening, or dress it up with a long black skirt for a special occasion. You could also make a tube top using this pattern by omitting the armbands and straps.

Materials:

6 (6, 7, 7, 8, 8, 9) balls (1.75 oz./50 g/136 yd. each) 100% mercerized cotton yarn in taupe

Size F/5 (3.75 mm) hook

Yarn needle

Sewing needle and matching thread

24" tiny elastic for strap (optional)

Fabric glue (optional)

Used in this project: Patons Grace yarn in Taupe, "Okay to Wash It" fabric glue

Gauge:

Having the right gauge is very important with this top. Change to a larger hook if the gauge does not match.

14 shell rows = 3½"

3 shell rows = 1¾"

7 sc = 2"

7 sc rows = 1"

1 three-leaf clover = 1"

Special Stitch:

Sc Shell (sh): In designated st, work (1 sc, ch 2, 1 sc).

Three-Leaf Clover (clo): (Ch 5, sl st in fifth ch from hook) 3 times.

INSTRUCTIONS:
Back

Row 1: Ch 81 (87, 93, 99, 105, 111) In third ch from hook, work (sc, ch 2, sc — shell made) * sk 2 chs, sh in next ch, rep from * across, ch 1, turn — 27 (29, 31, 33, 35, 39, 41) shs.

Row 2: Sh in each ch-2 sp of sh across, ch 1, turn.

Rows 3-14: (all sizes) Rep Row 2.

Note: If you are making sizes 1x or 2x, do not work dec rows. 1x and 2x will be worked even with 39 shells (1x) and 41 shells (2x) until piece measures 14" or desired length from beg ch to underarm.

Row 15: 2 sh dec row (sizes xs-xlg only should measure 3½" from beg ch at this point) sh in first sh; * in ch-2 sp of next sh, pull up a lp. 2 lps on hook, pull up a lp in ch 2 sp of next sh, yo and pull through all 3 lps on hook (1 sh dec made). * Ch 2, sc in same sh (third shell). Sh in next 21 (23, 25, 27, 29) shs. Repeat between * one time, sh in last sh, ch 1, turn — 25 (27, 29, 31, 33).

Rows 16-20 (xs-xlg): Work even with no dec — 25 (27, 29, 31, 33).

Row 21 (xs-xlg): Sh in first 7 shs, dec 1 sh over next 2 shs, sh in next 7 (9, 11, 13, 15) shs, dec 1 sh over next 2 shs, sh in next 7 shs, ch 1, turn (2 sh decs made), 23 (25, 27, 29, 31) shs.

Rows 22-36: (xs-xlg) Work even with no dec until piece measures 9".

Row 37 (xs-xlg — 2 sh inc row): Sh in first sh, sh in sp before next sh, (inc made) sh in next 21 (23, 25, 27, 29) shs, sh in sp before last sh (inc) sh in last sh, ch 1, turn — 25 (27, 29, 31, 33) shs.

Rows 38-40 (xs-xlg): Work even — 25 (27, 29, 31, 33) shs.

Row 41 (xs-xlg): 2 sh inc row) Rep row 37, working 23 (25, 27, 29, 31) shells after first inc, ch 1, turn — 27 (29, 31, 33, 35) shs.

Rows 42-54 (all sizes): Rep Row 2, working even until piece is 13" or desired length from beg ch to underarm. End off.

Front

(All sizes): Make same as back. With WS tog, sew side seams with yarn and yarn needle. Turn RS out.

Band for Top Edge

Attach yarn at either side to st at top of side seam on last row worked. Place 4 markers in ch-2 sp of 4 shs evenly spaced around top edge. Sc in each sh and in each st between shs; where markers were placed. Work 2sctog (dec) over marked st and next sc (4 dec made). Cont working in rnds without joining, until band measures 1¼" or desired width. End off.

Attaching Sleeve Band to Band on Top

Row 1: Working from WS of band on inside, attach yarn to st at top of band directly above side seam. Counting sl st as first ch, ch 44 (46, 48, 50, 52, 56, 58) being careful not to twist ch, turn front toward you and join to st next to where first sl st was placed, forming a circle; ch 1.

Row 2: Ch 1, sc in each sc around, join to first sc with sl st. Do not attach to band on top, allowing arm band to hang loosely. At this point, try top on to make sure band fits your arm. (You have the option of later weaving elastic through top row so band will not slide down.) If band is too tight, add to beg ch. Cont working scs in rnds till band measures approx. 1". Join with sl st. End off.

Dangling Cloverleafs

Cloverleaf 1: Turn arm band upside down and attach to center st of underarm on edge. Ch 6, work 3 leaf clo (see special st), sl st to ch before first clo leaf. End off.

Cloverleaf 2: Sk next st, attach yarn to next st, ch 11, work 3 leaf clo, sl st in ch before first clo leaf. End off. Cont around band. Rep Cloverleaf 1 and 2. End off. Rep for other band.

Optional elastic: On outside of armband at top edge, starting at seam, attach yarn to band and work scs all around top edge of band encasing elastic between sts. Be sure to leave long tails for tying tog. Try armband on and adjust to fit; tie knot in ends of elastic.

Straps

Try top on and pm on front and back where you want straps to be. On front, join yarn to st at marker, ch 57 and attach to back at marker. Try top on and adjust number of chs to fit. From inside (WS), sl st to st at left of where you joined, ch 1, turn. Encasing elastic between sts as you work, sc in each ch across and attach to edge of band. End off.

Optional: With yarn needle, weave elastic through strap. Adjust and sew ends to WS with needle and thread to secure.

Finishing

Weave in ends, and secure each end with fabric glue. Press cloverleaves flat if desired.

Skill Level — Advanced Beginner

LIGHT
3
LEGER
Ligero

Size xs-sm (med, lg, xlg, 1x, 2x, 3x)
Hip sizes — 34½"-37½ (38"-40", 41"-43", 44"-46½", 47"-49", 52"-57¾", 58"-61¼")

Skirt Overlay

This project is perfect if you want a crocheted skirt but don't have time to make one. It also looks great over a bathing suit.

INSTRUCTIONS:

Motifs

See materials for size hook to use for each skirt size.

Sizes xs-sm, med, lg: make 5 motifs.

Sizes xl, 1x: make 6 motifs.

Sizes 2x, 3x: make 7 motifs.

Ch 8, join with sl st to form a ring.

Rnd 1: Ch 3 (counts as first dc throughout), 27 more dc in ring, join to top of ch 3 — 28 dc.

Rnd 2: Ch 1, sc in same st as joining, * ch 4, sk next dc, sc in next dc, ch 10, sk next dc, sc in next dc, rep from * around. End with sl st in first sc, ch 1, turn — 7 ch-10 lps and 7 ch-4 lps.

Rnd 3: Sl st twice in ch-10 lp, ch 3, 4 dc in same lp, * ch 5, 5 dc in next ch-10 lp, rep from *. End with ch 5, join, ch 1, turn — 35 dc with ch-5 between each set.

Rnd 4: * Sl st into ch-5 sp, ch 10, sl st into same ch-5 sp, sl st into first dc of 5-dc group, ch 4, sl st into center dc, ch 4, sl st into last dc of 5-dc group, rep from *. End with sl st in first sl st. End off — 7 ch-10 lps, 14 ch-4 lps.

Next Step: Attach motifs with yarn, securing with 2 knots on underside at ch-10 lps on each side of motifs as in Diagram A. Before weaving in loose ends, place motifs around hip area over garment with which it will be worn. If piece is too small, add another motif. If it's too large, eliminate one motif (you may have to adjust length of chs between motifs).

Waistband

Row 1: Sl st to any ch-10 lp on any motif, * counting first sl st as first ch (here and throughout pattern), ch 13, attach with sl st to next ch-10 lp on motif, ch 11, attach to ch-10 lp on second motif. Rep from * with all 5 (6, 7) motifs, making sure you have 13 chs between petals and 11 chs between each motif. End last ch lp with ch 15 (instead of 13); ch 1, turn.

Row 2: Sc in second ch from hook and in each ch across, ch 1, turn.

Rows 3-4: Rep Row 2, working sc in each sc. At end of Row 4, end off.

Chain Links Below Motifs

Connect lower part of motifs.

Rnd 1: Attach yarn to any loose ch-10 lp (petal) that is at lower left side of any motif. * Ch 11, join to next ch-10 lp on next motif (connecting them tog), ch 15, join to next petal (twice), rep from * around, sl st to first sl st. End off. Ch 11 will only be between each motif.

Rnd 2: Attach yarn to center of any ch lp sp, * ch 15, sl st to next ch sp. Rep from * around, sl st to first sl st. End off.

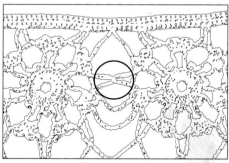

Diagram A

Materials:

1 ball (400 yd.) crochet cotton yarn or thread in linen

For sizes xs-sm, size G/6 (4 mm) hook

Med, size H/8 (5 mm) hook

Lg, size I/9 (5.5 mm) hook

Xlg, size H/8 (5 mm) hook

1x-2x, size I/9 (5.5 mm) hook

3x, size J/10 (6 mm) hook

1 button, ½" in diameter

Yarn needle

Sewing needle and matching thread

Used in this project: Aunt Lydia's Denim Quick Crochet Cotton yarn in Linen, "Okay To Wash It" fabric glue

Gauge:

Each motif (from 10" lp to 10" lp): (G = 7¼")
(H = 7¾") (I = 8¼")
(J = 8¾")

7 sc: (G = 1⅝")
(H = 1⅝") (I = 1¾")
(J = 1⅞") — waistband

2 dc: (G and H = ⅜")
(I and J = ½")

Helpful Hint:

Placing connected motifs around a form, such as a dark throw pillow, will help when working chains together for the waistband.

Words of Encouragement

There are times when children don't want to listen to their parents. It may seem as if they are constantly giving you a hard time about things you will not allow them to do. But your children are listening and they need guidelines to feel that you love them, even if they fuss about it. When I was in high school I had a friend whose parents let her do just about anything she wanted. Once she told me, "Mary Jane, sometimes I just wish they would say no. Then I would know that they really loved me."

Rnd 3: Rep Rnd 2, working ch-16 lp instead of ch-15 lp. End off.

Rnd 4: Pm at first sl st, and repeating Rnd 2, work ch 17, instead of ch 15. At last lp, instead of ch 17, work ch 14 (so sp won't be so big), attach ch 14 to first ch-17 on rnd. Cont working ch-17 sps in rnds without ending off until desired length. End off.

Fill-in Stitches Between Motifs

Step 1: Attach yarn to lower ch-4 sp on any motif, as in Diagram B. Ch 15, being careful not to twist ch, attach to corresponding ch-4 sp on next motif. End off.

Step 2: Attach yarn to ch-4 sp directly above ch-4 sp in first step, ch 10 and attach to ch-4 on next motif. End off. Rep Steps 1 and 2 on all other motifs.

Step 3: Turn piece upside down. At-tach yarn to center st on underside of waistband at open sp between motifs, as in Diagram B, ch 9 and attach to ch-4 sp closest to ch-10 sp at center of motif at rt as in Diagram B. End off.

Step 4: Attach yarn to same center sp on waistband as in Step 3, ch 9 and attach to ch-4 to motif at rt. End off. Rep Steps 1-4 between each motif.

Finishing — Button and Loop

Attach yarn to either corner on long loose end of waistband, ch 7, attach to other corner, ch 1, turn, work 7 sc around ch-7, sl st to edge of waistband. End off. Sew button to top of waistband on opposite side at other end.

Fringe: Attach three 14" pieces of yarn that have been folded in half to each ch-17 sp on bottom row for fringe. Trim ends even. Weave in end.

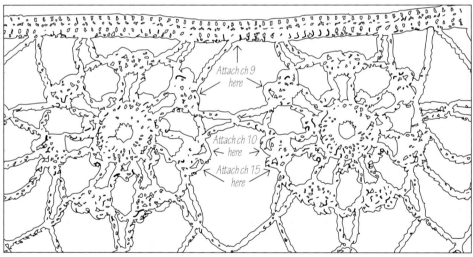

Attach ch 9 here

Attach ch 10 here

Attach ch 15 here

Diagram B

One size fits most

Lace Bangle Bracelet

Are you in a rut and bored with your crochet? If you are the kind of person who makes only afghans or scarves, and you use only yarn, then why not break out of your comfort zone and do something new? Try this crocheted bracelet with bedspread cotton thread — it's not as hard as you think!

Materials:

1 ball (150 yd.) #10 cotton thread in cream

Size D/3 (3.25 mm) hook

1½"-wide bangle bracelet

Tacky glue

Yarn needle

Used in this project: J&P Coats Knit-Cro-Sheen

Gauge:

2 sc = ⅜"

1 shell = 1"

INSTRUCTIONS:
Piece for Inside of Bracelet

Row 1: Ch 51, sc in second ch from hook and in each across — 50 sc.

Rows 2-7: Sc in each sc across, ch 1, turn. You may have to work more or less rows for piece to come out a little over the edge on each side. End off.

Next Step: Glue piece to inside of bracelet, keeping edges free from glue so you can attach thread and work extra rows. Make sure ends meet. Let dry.

Outside of Bracelet
Work in rnds.

Attach thread to one side of bracelet at first st on row (at corner).

Rnd 1: Increasing 10 sc, evenly spaced, sc around entire edge, attach to first sc with sl st. You will make incs about every fifth sc — 60 sc.

Rnd 2: * Ch 5, sk 3 sc, 1 sc in next ch, rep from * around, sl st to first sc — 15 ch-5 sps.

Rnd 3: Ch 5, sc in first ch-5 sp, * 7 dc in next ch-5 sp, sc in next ch-5 sp, ch 5, sc in next ch-5 sp, rep from * around. End with sc in last ch-5 sp, sl st in sc at base of first ch-5 sp made at beg of rnd. This is done so this ch-5 sp looks like the others. 5 7-dc shells and 1 ch-5 sp between each sh.

Rnd 4: Sl st to center of ch-5 sp, ch 5, sk next (sc and dc), * sc in next dc, (which is second dc of sh), ch 5, sk 3 dc. Sc in next dc, ch 5, sk (1 dc and 1 sc) 1 sc in next ch 5 sp, ch 5, sk next sc and next dc, rep from *. End with sl st to center of first ch-5 sp of Rnd 3. You should have 2 ch-5 sps between each sh and 1 ch-5 sp above each sh — 15 ch-5 sps total.

Rnd 5: Rep Rnd 3.

Rnd 6: Rep Rnd 4.

Rnd 7: Attach thread with sl st to sc at loose edge, * sl st across next 2 sc on loose edge, sl st next ch-5 sp to next sc, rep from * around, sl st to first sc on loose edge, securing in place. End off.

Finishing
Weave in all loose ends. For a 1"-wide bracelet, eliminate rows to fit.

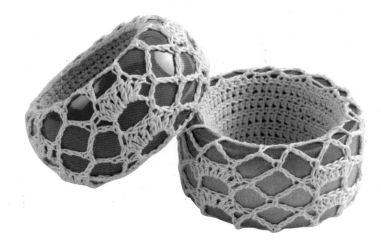

Size — sm-med (lg, xlg)

MEDIUM
4
MOYEN
Medio

Tie-Front Sweater

Doubling the yarn and using chain link stitches will help you create this trendy sweater in no time! Instructions are also given to make it cropped like a shrug.

Materials:

3 skeins (10 oz./283 g/ 508 yd. per skein) yarn in variegated blue

Size H/8 (5 mm) or size K/10.5 (6.5 mm) hook

Yarn needle

Used in this project: Caron Rainbow Dreams in Jet Stream, used with crochet hook size H (5 mm). Substitute 3 skeins (6 oz. each) Caron Simply Soft, used with crochet hook size K (6.5 mm).

Gauge:

Measure gauge on fourth row.

(sc, ch-3 lp, sc, ch-3 lp, sc) = 3"

1 ch-3 lp = 1¼"

4 ch-3 rows = 2"

INSTRUCTIONS:

Note: Use 2 strands of yarn for yoke and sleeves, but only 1 strand for flare at sleeve ends, ties and lower bodice.

The starting ch is the waistline of bodice of sweater.

Top Bodice Front

With 2 strands of yarn and H hook (or K hook, depending on yarn used), loosely ch 61 (65, 69).

Row 1: Sc in second ch from hook and in each ch across, turn — 60 (64, 68) sc.

Row 2: * Ch 3, skip first sc, sc in next sc, rep from * across row, turn — 30 (32, 34) ch-3 lps.

Row 3: * Ch 3, sc in next ch-3 lp, rep from * across, turn — 30 (32, 34) lps.

Row 4-8: Rep Row 3 — 30 (32, 34) lps.

Row 9: Ch 2, sc in first lp, * ch 3, sc in next lp, rep from * across row, end with sc in last lp, turn — 29 (31, 33) lps.

Row 10: This is Row 1 of left front. This row will start to divide the bodice for underarm. Ch 2, sc in first lp (ch 3, sc in next lp) 6 (7, 8) times, turn. 7 (8, 9) lps on this row, which includes 6 (7, 8) ch-3 lps, and 1 ch-2 lp.

Row 11 (Row 2 of left front): Shape armhole: sl st to center of first ch-3 lp, * ch 3, sc in next lp, rep from * across, end with last sc in ch-2 lp, turn — 6 (7, 8) lps (includes ch 2 lp).

Row 12 (Row 3 of left front): Ch 2, sc in first ch-3 lp. Work in patt as established, turn — 6 (7, 8) lps.

Rows 13-16: Rep last 2 rows twice — 4 (5, 6) lps.

Row 17 (Row 8 of left front): Ch 2, sc in first space, * ch 3, sc in next sp, rep from * across. End with sc in ch-2 lp — 4 (5, 6) lps.

Rows 18-25: Rep Row 17. End off.

Top Bodice Back

Row 1: With 2 strands, join yarn to same sp at left underarm with last lp of front, * ch 3, sc in next sp, rep from * 14 (15, 16) times, turn — 15 (16, 17) lps.

Row 2: Sl st to center of first ch-3 lp, * ch 3, sc in next lp, rep from * across, turn — 14 (15, 16) lps. Rep Row 2, decreasing in the following manner:

Row 3: 13 (14, 15) lps.

Row 4: 12 (13, 14) lps.

Row 5: 11 (12, 13) lps.

Rows 6-13: Work even with no decs, being sure to ch 3 at beg of each row.

Neck Shaping and Shoulders

Row 14 of back: Work 4 (5, 6) lps, turn.

Rows 15-16: Work 4 (5, 6) lps. End off.

Other side of rows 14-16: Turn work, and join yarn to first lp on row at short side of back at armhole, ch 3, work 4 lps. Turn and work 2 more rows even, same as other side. End off.

Right Front of Top Bodice

At unworked edge of rt center front, join yarn and ch 2. Work rt front same as left front, reversing shaping. End off — 25 rows total. Sew shoulder seams.

Sleeves
Make 2, begin at lower edge.

With 2 strands, ch 18 (20, 22). Join to first ch to form a ring. Mark beg of first rnd.

Rnd 1: Ch 3, sc in next ch, * ch 3, sk next ch, sc in next ch, rep from * around. Join to top of ch 3 with sl st from here on out — 9 (10, 11) ch-3 lps.

Rnds 2-11: * Ch 3, sc in next lp, rep from * around — 9 (10, 11) lps on each rnd.

Rnd 12 (inc rnd): Ch 3, sc in last ch-3 lp worked in, work in patt around. (1 lp inc — 10 (11, 12) lps on this rnd.) You'll be working 2 scs, with a ch-3 lp in between, in the first lp of the inc rnd.

Rnds 13-23: Work even with no incs.

Rnd 24 (inc rnd): Rep Rnd 12 — 11 (12, 13) lps.

Rnds 25-35: Work even with no incs.

Rnd 36 (inc rnd): Rep Rnd 12 — 12 (13, 14) lps.

Rnds 37-38: Work even.

Armhole Shaping for Sleeve Cap
Rnd 39: Ch 2, sc in next ch-3 lp, * ch 3, sc in next ch-3 lp, rep from * 9 (10, 11) times, turn — 11 (12, 13) lps (includes ch-2 lp).

Rnd 40: Ch 2, sc in next ch-3 lp, * ch 3, sc in next ch-3 lp, rep from * to within last ch 2-lp, turn (do not sc in last ch-2 lp) — 10 (11, 12) lps.

Rnds 41-46: Rep last rnd 6 (7, 8) times. End off — 4 lps (all sizes).

Flared Rounds for Sleeve End
At wrist: 1 strand of yarn and H (or K, if using Simply Soft) hook.

Rnd 1: Sl st into any sc on sleeve edge. * Ch 3, sk next st, sc in next st, rep from * around — 9 (10, 11) ch-3 lps.

Rnds 2-11: Inc 1 lp every other rnd, or until you reach desired length for flared sleeve. End off. Rnd 11 should have 14 (15, 16) ch-3 lps.

Example — Rnd 2: Inc 1 lp this rnd (10 lps). Rnd 3: Work even (10 lps). Rnds 4 and 5 should each have 11 lps, etc.

RS tog, sew sleeves onto sweater with yarn and needle.

Edging
Step 1 (back): With RS facing and size K hook (all sizes), attach 1 strand of yarn to first st at left lower corner, sc in same st as sl st, sc in each st across lower back edge — 60 (64, 68) sc.

Step 2 (rt center front): 2 sc in each of next 2 sc (corner) Cont up rt center front edge, sc 28 sts evenly across to rt shoulder seam.

Step 3 (neck): Cont across neck edge, sc 28 (30, 32) evenly across to next shoulder seam.

Step 4 (Left center front): Cont down left center front, work 28 sc evenly across to left corner at bottom of sweater, 2 sc in each of last 2 sts for corner.

Helpful Hint:
On flared sleeve, pm at each inc, and when you work inc on 2 rnds above that, move inc over to the left 1-2 lps. Do not place incs above each other — stagger them.

Ties

Note: For shorter ties, work fewer rows.

Row 1: With 1 strand of yarn and K hook, attach yarn to st at front rt corner. Sc in same sp as joining, sc in next sc, ch 1, turn — 2 sc.

Row 2: 1 sc in each sc, ch 1, turn — 2 sc.

Rows 3-46: Rep Row 2. End off. Rep for other side.

Finishing Edge

(Work around entire shrug and ties).

With RS facing, take 1 strand of yarn and H hook, and attach yarn to first sc at left side of tie on left lower front, counting sl st as first ch, ch 3, sk 1 sc, sc in next sc, * ch 3, sk next sc, sc in next sc, rep from * across lower back edge — 30 (32, 34) ch-3 lps.

Next Step: Cont up side of tie, * ch 3, skip 2 rows, sc in next row (or space) rep from * ending with sc in sc on row 46 of tie. Ch 3, sc in second sc on end — 23 ch-3 lps on side edge of tie and 1 ch-3 lp at end of tie.

Next Step: Cont up other side of tie, * ch 3, sk 2 rows, sc in next sp, rep from * cont up rt front, neck, and left front edges, sc and ch 3 around next tie in same manner. At end of tie, sl st to first sl st. End off — 168 (172, 176) ch-3 lps around entire edge of sweater, including ties. You can end here for a cropped top, or go to the next step to extend the length.

Body of Top Below Yoke (all sizes)

Row 1: With 1 strand, attach yarn to last ch 3 at bottom edge of tie at left corner of top, * ch 4, sc in next ch-3 lp, rep from * across, end with ch 4 in first ch-3 lp at rt corner of top, ch 5, turn.

Rows 2-13: Sc to first ch-4 lp, * ch 5, sc to next ch-4 lp, rep from * across, ch 5, turn. Rep Row 2 until you have reached desired length.

Helpful Hint:
If you are using a stiff, acrylic yarn, put it in the dryer with fabric sheets to make it softer.

This sweater also looks great in raspberry.

Finished size — Scarf on one side is 28" long from bottom edge of cap

Skill Level — Advanced Beginner

MEDIUM
4
MOYEN
Medio

Darling Daisy Hat/Scarf

Girls and women of all ages love flowers! Encourage someone by making this cute hat/scarf combination to brighten her day. You can also add crocheted flowers to ready-made clothing for a quick, fresh update.

Materials:

2 skeins (3 oz./85 g/ 158 yd.) wool yarn in cadet blue (A)

1 skein (3 oz./85 g/ 158 yd.) each wool yarn in green (B), pink (C) and yellow (D)

Size I/9 (5.5 mm) and C/2 (2.75 mm) hooks

Sewing needle and thread in cadet blue

Yarn needle

Used in this project: Lion Brand Wool yarn in Cadet blue, Sage and Rose, and Lamb's Pride worsted in Lemon Drop

Gauge:

5 hdc and 4 hdc rows = 1½"

1 ch-5 lp and 1 ch link row = 1¼"

Large flower = 3½"

Small flower = 1½"

INSTRUCTIONS:
Hat

Rnd 1: With color A, ch 4, sl st to first ch to form ring, ch 2 (counts as first hdc throughout patt). Work 9 hdc in ring, changing to new color (B) in last st (hdc) in this manner: Work last st (hdc) of row until 3 lps (color A) are left on hook; drop yarn in use. With next color (B), draw through all 3 lps on hook. Cont with new color, sl st(ing) new color to top of ch 2 (at bg of rnd) from here to end. Cut previous color, leaving 4" tail — 10 hdc.

Rnd 2: Ch 2, hdc in same sp, 2 hdc (inc) in each hdc around, on last hdc change to color C (in same manner as Rnd 1), sl st to ch 2 — 20 hdc.

Rnd 3: Ch 2, 2 hdc in next hdc; * hdc in next hdc, 2 hdc in next hdc, rep from * around, change to B, sl st to ch 2 — 30 hdc.

Rnd 4: Ch 2, hdc in next hdc, 2 hdc in next hdc, * hdc in each of next 2 hdc, 2 hdc in next hdc, rep from * around, change to B, sl st to ch 2 — 40 hdc.

Rnd 5: Cont in patt and color sequence, counting ch 2 as first hdc and working 3 hdc between each inc — 50 hdc.

Rnd 6: Work 9 hdc between incs — 55 hdc.

Rnd 7: Work 9 hdc between incs, end with hdc in las 5 hdc — 60 hdc.

Rnds 8-19: Work even with no incs. End off at end of Rnd 19 — 60 hdc.

Attached Scarf

Row 1: Fold hat, and lay flat — 30 hdc each side. With crown toward you and hat edge away from you, count 13 sts in center at bottom edge of hat. Pm at first st to rt and to thirteenth st to left. With A, attach yarn to first st, * ch 5, sk 2 chs, sl st in next ch, rep from * 3 more times. End with last sl st in thirteenth st where marker was placed, ch 5, turn — 4 ch-5 lps.

Row 2: Sc in first ch-5 sp, * ch 5, sc in next ch-5 sp, rep from * across, ch 5, turn — 4 lps.

Rows 3-44: Rep Row 2. End off, leaving an 8" tail. Rep on other side of hat.

Large Flower
Make 4 with C.

Rnd 1: Ch 2; in second ch, work 8 sc, sl st to first sc — 8 sc.

Rnd 2: * Ch 10, sl st in same sp, sl st in next sc, rep from *, around. Sl st to first sl st, (sl st to next ch-10 lp, 11

sc in ch-10 lp) 8 times, join to first sl st. End off. Pull tail in center to tighten — 8 ch-10 lps. For yellow center (make 4), with C hook, ch 2, 7 sc in second ch from hook, sl st to first sc. End off. Weave ends into center of flower, and tie in back.

Small Flowers
Make 6 in B, 4 in C and 4 in D.

Rnd 1: With C hook, ch 2; in second ch, work 6 sc, sl st to first sc — 6 sc.

Rnd 2: * Ch 5, sl st to next sc, rep from * around, sl st to first sl st. End off — 6 ch-5 lps.

Finishing
Gather bottom edge of scarf with yarn needle and 8" tail; tie to secure. With loose ends, attach daisy to gathered edge of scarf. Sew lps of daisy to scarf with needle and thread. Pm on scarf where you want small flowers, and sew to scarf with needle and thread. Sew daisy to scarf right below edge of hat. Rep on other side.

Helpful Hint:
If your loose end is too short to weave in, weave the needle through the stitches first. Then, place the yarn through the eye and pull it through the stitches.

Size xs-med (lg-xlg, 1x-2x)

BULKY
5
BULKY
Abultado

Angel Hair Bolero

This is basically a vest pattern with sleeves added, so you can make either one. The sleeves are worked right onto the armhole, making it an easy project if you do not like to sew in sleeves. The angel hair yarn is some of the softest yarn I have ever touched! It's heavenly!

INSTRUCTIONS:

Begins at lower edge. Back and fronts are worked in one piece before adding sleeves. See Diagram A.

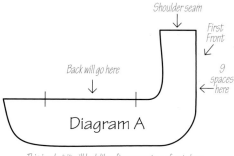

Diagram A

This is what it will look like after you get one front done, before you do the back.

With H (J, M) hook, loosely ch 80 to measure 26" (30", 36").

Row 1: Dc in sixth ch from hook (counts as first dc + ch 1), * ch 1, sk 1 ch, dc in next ch. Rep from * across row, ch 4, turn — 38 spaces + 39 dc (mark this as RS).

Row 2: Sk first dc, (dc, ch 1 and dc) in next dc (1 sp inc), * ch 1, dc in next dc. Rep from * across to last dc, dc, ch 1, dc in last dc (1 sp inc). Ch 1, dc in fourth ch of tch, ch 4, turn — 40 sps + 41 dc.

Row 3: Rep Row 2, working last dc in third ch of tch, ch 4, turn — 42 sps + 43 dc.

Rows 4-8: Work evenly in patt.

Divide for Fronts and Back

For clarity, start counting here as Row 1 of front.

Row 9 (Row 1 of front): Work in patt until 9 sps and 10 dc have been made; ch 3, turn. See Diagram A.

Front

Row 10 (Row 2 of front): Work even in this manner: Sk first ch-1 sp, dc in next dc, work in patt across, with ch 1 between each dc, end with last dc in top of tch, ch 4, turn — 9 sps + 10 dc.

Row 11 (Row 3 of front): Dec row — work 7 sps across, ch 1, 2dctog, ch 3, turn — 8 sps.

Rows 12-17 (Rows 4-9 of front): Cont to dec 1 sp at arm side in this manner, every other row, until 5 sps remain (You will dec on Rows 5, 7, and 9 of front) Rows 5 and 6 will have 7 sps, Rows 7 and 8 will have 6 sps, Row 9 will have 5 sps. Make sure the ch 4s are at the outside front edge and the ch 3s are at the armhole edge.

Rows 18-20 (Rows 10-12 of front): Start ch 4 on each end here: Work even. End off.

Back

Row 1 (same row as Row 1 of front and Row 9 of body): Sk 4 sps from section just worked, for armhole (see Diagram B). Join yarn in next dc, ch 4, work until 16 sps have been made — 17 dc including ch 4.

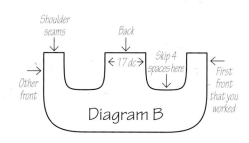

Diagram B

Next Step: Work rows even in patt until back is same length as left and rt armhole.

Materials:

3 (4, 4) skeins (3.5 oz./ 100 g/120 yd. each) yarn in purple

For xs-med, size H/8 (5 mm) hook

For lg-xlg, size J/10 (6 mm)

For 1x-2x, size M/13 (9 mm)

Used in this project: Jo-Ann Sensations Angel Hair yarn in purple

Gauge:

Note: Number of sts is the same for all sizes. Gauge determines size, and is very important with this project, so if gauge does not match, change your hook.

3 dc + 3 ch 1 =

(H hook, 2")

(J hook, 2¼")

(M hook, 2¾")

3 dc rows = 2" (2½", 3").

To decrease 1 space (2dctog) yo, insert hook into next dc and pull up lp on hook (3 lps on hook). Yo again and pull through 2 lps, (2 lps on hook). Yo, insert hook in next dc, and pull up lp on hook (4 lps on hook). Yo and pull yarn through 2 lps (3 lps on hook). Yo and pull through 3 rem lps on hook.

Helpful Hint:

If you are a beginner, choose a light-colored yarn for your first project. It is harder to see stitches with a dark yarn.

Second front: On RS starting at front edge, attach yarn and ch 4. Work second front in same manner as first front. With yarn and yarn needle, sew shoulder seams with RS tog.

Sleeves
Work in rounds.

Rnd 1 of sleeve: With RS facing you, attach yarn to dc in center of under-arm hole, ch 4, work 27 sps and 27 dc evenly spaced around armhole edge. Join to ch 3 of ch 4. Ch 4, but do not turn. Pm at beg of each rnd.

Rnds 2-5: Work even in patt.

Rnd 6: Dec 1 sp at end of rnd (last 2dctog), 26 sps and 26 dc.

Rnd 7: Dec 1 sp at beg of rnd (first 2dctog), 25 sps and 25 dc.

Rnds 7-13: Cont to dec 1 sp each rnd, alternating in this manner: 2dctog at end of rnd, then work the dec at the beg on the next rnd. You should have 19 sps on Rnd 13.

Rnds 14-22: Work even with no dec — 19 sps.

Rnd 23: Work even. End off — 19 sps.

Rnd 24: Sc in same sp, and in each dc and ch-1 around. End off — 38 sc.

Rep on other sleeve.

Finishing Edge
With RS of bolero facing you, join yarn at top left front edge (first sp on shoulder front). Ch 4, sl st in side of next sp, * ch 4, sl st in side of next sp, rep from * around bottom left curved edge. Ch 3, and sl st in each ch-1 sp at bottom back edge of bolero. When you get to the next curved edge (bottom rt front), start ch 4 and sl st, instead of ch 3s. Cont up RS edge. (Ch 3 and sl st) in each ch-1 sp of back neck edge. End off.

MEDIUM
4
MOYEN
Medio

Finished size — 5¼" x 55" without fringe

Coffee Lover's Scarf

If you enjoy coffee, you'll love this scarf (and get lots of compliments at the coffee shop)! One of my favorite things in life is getting together with a friend to share a hot cup of coffee.

Materials:

1 ball (3 oz./85 g/197 yd.) yarn in brown

1 ball each mercerized 100% cotton crochet thread #3 in red (A) and brown (B)

1 skein each 6-strand embroidery thread in taupe and blue

Size I/9 (5.5 mm) hook for scarf

US steel hook size 5 (1.7 mm) for coffee cup

Yarn needle

Sewing needle and matching thread

Used in this project: Lion Brand Wool Ease in Mink Brown (MC), and DMC Color Variations embroidery floss #3782, #3808 and #3790 for diamonds. If using #10, it needs to be doubled.

Gauge:

Scarf: 7 dc = 2" (with I hook)

3 dc rows = 2"

Cup and saucer = 4" x 3½" with handle (with steel hook)

7 sc and 8 sc rows = 1"

Helpful Hint:

People tend to crochet more tightly when they are stressed and loosely when they are relaxed. So if days or weeks go by before you pick up a project again, make sure your gauge is still the same.

INSTRUCTIONS:
Coffee Cup
Make 2.

Row 1: With steel hook and color A, ch 9, sc in second ch from hook, and in each ch across, ch 1, turn — 8 sc.

Row 2: 2 sc in first sc (inc) sc in each sc to within last sc, 2 sc in last sc, ch 1, turn — 10 sc.

Rows 3-6: Rep Row 2 — 18 sc on Row 6.

Row 7: Work even — 18 sc.

Rows 8-9: Rep Row 2 — 22 sc on Row 9.

Rows 10-11: Work even — 22 sc.

Row 12: Rep Row 2 — 24 sc.

Rows 13-18: Work even, at end of Row 18, ch 3 — 24 sc on Row 18.

Row 19: * Dc in first sc, hdc in next 3 sc, sc in next 2 sc, sl st in next 2 sc. End off.

Other end of Row 19: Turn piece over and attach thread to first sc on un-worked end, ch 3, rep from *. End off.

Brown Coffee
Row 1: With (B), attach to second st on top row (Row 19), ch 1, sc in next 21 sts, sl st in next st, leaving last st unworked. Ch 1, turn.

Row 2: Sk first st, sl st in next st, sc in next 19 sc, sl st in next st, ch 1, turn.

Row 3: Sk first 2 sts, sl st in next st, sc in next 2 sts, hdc in next 10 sts, sc in next 2 sts, sl st in next 2 sts, ch 1, turn.

Row 4: Sk first 2 sts, sl st in next st, sc in next 7 sts, sl st in next 2 sts. End off.

Red Brim
Row 1: Attach (A) to st on last red row (to rt of brown), ch 1, sc in same sp, sc in blo of next 21 brown sts. End with sl st in red at edge of coffee cup. End off — 22 sc.

Handle
Attach (A) to end of Row 10 at rt edge, ch 16, sk 9 sts, sl st to next st on side edge of cup, ch 1, turn, * 2 sc in next ch, 1 sc in next ch, rep from *. End with 1 sc in last st, sl st to side edge of cup. End off — 24 sc.

Saucer
Make 2.

Rnd 1: Ch 26, sc in second ch from hook, sc in next ch, * hdc in next ch, dc in next 19 chs, hdc in next ch, sc in next 2 chs —25 sc. Ch 1 (loosely), working on opp. side, sc in first 2 sc, rep from * across row. End with sc in last 2 chs; do not turn.

Rnd 2: Ch 2 (loosely), cont around other side, sk first st, * sl st in next st. Sc in next st, hdc in next st, dc in next 16 sts, hdc in next st, sc in next st, sl st in next st. End off. On other side, attach to second st from end (at rt), rep from *. End off.

Words of Encouragement

Do you have many friends in your life? If you feel alone, maybe it's because you are just waiting for someone to call or have you over. Start reaching out to other people instead of waiting for them to reach out to you. I know you have heard the saying, "If you want to have friends, you have to be a friend." Have someone over for coffee, and maybe a friendship will start to grow.

Diamonds

Make 2 teal and 1 brown for each cup.

Row 1: With steel hook and 3 strands embroidery thread, ch 2, 2 sc in second sc from hook, ch 1, turn — 2 sc.

Row 2: 2 sc in first sc, 2 sc in last sc, ch 1, turn — 4 sc.

Row 3: 2 sc in first sc, sc in next 2 sc, 2 sc in last sc, ch 1, turn — 6 sc.

Row 4: 2 sc in first sc, sc in next 4 sc, 2 sc in last sc, ch 1, turn — 8 sc.

Row 5: 2sctog (see pg. 9) over first 2 sc (dec worked), sc in next 4 sc, 2sctog over last 2 sc — 6 sc.

Row 6: 2sctog over first 2 sc, sc in next 2 sc, 2sctog over last 2 sc — 4 sc.

Row 7: 2sctog over first 2 sc, 2sctog over last 2 sc — 2 sc.

Row 8: 2sctog over last 2 sc.

Scarf

Row 1: With I hook and MC yarn, ch 20, dc in fourth ch from hook and in each ch across, ch 2 (counts as first st from now on), turn — 18 dc.

Row 2: Dc in each st across, ch 2, turn — 18 dc.

Rep Row 2 until scarf is 55" long. End off.

Finishing

Weave in ends. Sew diamonds to cup with sewing needle and 1 strand thread. Sew cups to ends of scarf. With embroidery thread, stitch steam onto scarf with an outline st (see Diagram A), as in photo. For fringe, cut 72 strands of yarn (14" each). Fold 2 strands of yarn and attach to st at end of scarf. Rep with other strands and on other end of scarf.

Diagram A

Work from left to right, keeping thread always on same side of needle, either to the left or right of it. Bring needle out where last stitch went in, following the line, which may be curved or straight.

FINE
2
FIN
Fino

Fits sizes xs (sm, med, lg, xlg, 1x, 2x), 28" long (all sizes)

Long, Lacy Tunic

A larger project like this may seem like a burden if you are used to making only small things. But just keep working at it, a little every day, and you'll be finished before you know it. You will be surprised at how easy this is!

INSTRUCTIONS:

Front
Ch 61 (66, 71, 76, 81, 91, 96), should measure 16½" (17½", 18½", 19½", 20½", 22½", 23½") when slightly stretched.

Row 1: [Work V-st (dc, ch 2, dc) into eighth ch from hook, * ch 3, sk 4 chs, work V-st into next ch] rep from * to last 3 chs, ch 2, 1 dc into last ch, turn — 11 (12, 13, 14, 15, 17, 18) V-sts, with dc at each end of row.

Row 2: Ch 4 (counts as 1 tr), sk first ch 2 sp, work 5 tr into next ch 2 sp, * sk ch 3 sp, work 5 tr into next ch 2 sp of V-st; rep from * to last sp, sk ch 2, 1 tr into next ch, turn — 11 (12, 13, 14, 15, 17, 18) shs.

Row 3: Ch 5, into middle tr of 5 tr sh work V-st, * ch 3, sk 4 tr, into next tr work V-st, rep from * to last 3 tr, ch 2, 1 dc into fourth ch of ch 4 at beg of prev row, turn.

Rows 4-28: Rep Rows 2 and 3. End off.

Left Sleeve and Left Shoulder
Row 1: With front facing, [attach yarn with sl st to corner at top of ch 4, before first sh. Loosely ch 26 (if you want the sleeve longer, do chs in increments of 5). Rep instructions in brackets on Row 1 of top front. Continue working V-sts across remainder of ch. When you come to end of ch 26 (where sl st was attached at corner), work V-st into same sp where yarn was attached to corner, ch 3 and cont in patt until you have worked over 4 (4, 5, 5, 6, 7, 7) shs. (You will have 5 V-sts across ch 26.) After you've worked last V-st, ch 2 and work 1 dc into top of fifth tr of same sh, turn

— 9 (9, 10, 10, 11, 12, 12) V-sts.

Row 2: Ch 4, cont in patt, to last sp, sk ch 2, tr into next ch, turn — 9 (9, 10, 10, 11, 12, 12) shs.

Rows 3-8: Work in patt, end with last row a sh row. End off.]

Note: for sizes sm-med, work 9 rows; sizes lg-xlg, 10 rows, and 1x-2x, 11 rows.

Right Front Shoulder and Sleeve
With WS facing, at opp corner (rt front), rep instructions in brackets on Rows 1-8 of left sleeve.

Back
Work same as front Rows 1-28.

Back Shoulder and Sleeves
Row 1: With back facing, attach yarn to top left corner, loosely ch 21. End off. Attach yarn to corner at rt, ch 26 and work same as Row 1 of left sleeve; do not end off after V-sts are worked. Work across first 4 shs of top row. After fourth V-st is worked, do not ch 2 and do not work dc in fifth tr of sh. After fourth V-st, ch 3 and cont in patt (V-st in center tr of next sh, etc.) across row. When you get to last sh at corner, work a V-st into corner as before, where yarn was attached. Work 4 V-sts across ch, skipping 4 chs between each. After last V-st, ch 1, sk 2 chs, dc in last ch, turn — 21 (22, 23, 24, 25, 27, 28) V-sts.

Row 2: Ch 4, cont in tr sh patt across row. End with sk dc, sk ch 1, tr into next ch, turn — 21 (22, 23, 24, 25, 27, 28).

Rows 3-9: Rep Rows 2 and 3 of front, ending with V-st row (Row 3). End off.

Materials:
3 (4, 4, 5, 5, 6, 7) skeins (3.52 oz./100 g/ 218 yd. each) sport-wt. 100% mercerized cotton yarn in blue

Size G/6 (4 mm) hook

Yarn needle

Used in this project: Sinfonia 100% mercerized cotton (available at Hobby Lobby and www.craftsetc.com). Substitute Paton's Grace.

Gauge:
9 sc = 2"

6 sc rows = 1¼"

1 5-tr shell = 1½" at widest point

1 dc V-st = ¾" at widest point

4 rows (2 tr sh rows with V-st rows between) = 2½"

Special Stitch:
V-Stitch: (1 dc, ch 2, 1 dc) in one st.

Tr Shell (tr sh): 5 triple crochet sts in designated st.

Helpful Hint:

This fitted tunic is very flattering, but if you want it to be loose, make the next larger size. You could also lengthen the tunic, add a belt, and wear it as a dress!

Words of Encouragement
We all carry burdens from time to time. But there are times we carry them unnecessarily. If someone tries to put a guilt trip on you, gives unjustified negative criticism, or tells a lie about you, it can feel like someone is stabbing you in the heart. If their words or actions are unjust, let it be their burden. Just because someone throws something at you doesn't means you have to catch it and carry it around. Choose not to let that person control you. Drop that burden and quit carrying it around like a ton of bricks on your shoulders!

Note: For sizes sm-med, work 10 rows; sizes lg-xlg, 11 rows, sizes 1x-2x, 12 rows.

Side and Shoulder Seams

Sew side and shoulder seams with yarn and yarn needle, matching up patt.

Arm Bands

Row 1: Attach yarn to seam at underarm on sleeve edge, sc in same sp, * work 2sctog (see pg. 9) over next 2 sts, sc in next st, rep from * around, sl st to first sc.

Row 2: Place 4 markers evenly spaced around armband. Work a dec over each marked sc and next st; sc in all other sts.

Rows 3-15: Pm at beg of row, and sc around continuously, without joining rows. End off.

Bottom Band

(Sc loosely so band is not too tight.)

Attach yarn to side seam at bottom edge, sc in same sp, sc in each st around, sl st to first sc.

Cont working evenly in rnds for 13-15 rows until band measures 2¾" wide. End off.

Neck Band

Rnd 1: With RS of back facing you, attach yarn to center back neck edge, sc in same sp, sc around neck, keeping neck edge flat. Working 2sctog in each corner (shoulder seams and neck front), sl st to first sc (4 decs).

Rnd 2: Ch 1, sc in same sp, sc around, working 2sctog at front 2 corners only. End off (2 decs). Weave in ends.

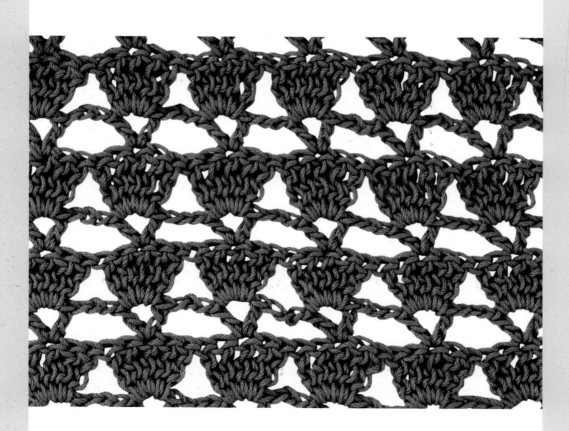

One size fits all

Candy-Colored Bracelet

This is a fun bracelet to make and to wear. Try crocheting it in other colors or as a necklace for more jewelry options.

Materials:

- 1 ball (150 yd.) each 4 different colors #3 crochet cotton thread
- US steel hook #5 (1.7 mm)
- 16" dangles (½"- ¾" each) or can substitute buttons
- White elastic cord or clear stretch plastic thread for beading
- 3 wooden or plastic ¾" beads
- Sewing needle with eye large enough for elastic to go through
- Yarn needle

Used in this project: J&P Coats Royale Fashion Crochet Thread, Favorite Findings shelly #1838

Gauge:

3 sc = ¼"

INSTRUCTIONS:

Curlique

For sm-med wrist, make 13; for lg-xlg wrist, make 16 (3-4 of each color).

Ch 15, 2 sc in second ch from hook, and 2 sc in each ch across. End off. Tie loose ends tog. Rep with other colors. If you want a shorter curlique, work fewer beg chs.

Ball

Make 3-4 (in different colors).

Ch 2, 8 sc in second ch, sl st to first sc, cont working in rnds, without joining. You'll need to inc some sts toward center of bead. Put bead inside to make sure it fits. After the halfway mark and toward the top, dec some rnds until the hole is closed up. End off.

To Assemble

Lay pieces on a table in the order to be placed on bracelet. Place round shells, balls and curliques onto elastic with needle. Make sl knot and ch 1, * pull up pink shell, ch 1 around it, ch 1; rep from *, alternating shells, balls and curliques until you have enough pieces to fit around wrist. Leave an 8" tail on each end of elastic. Tie loose ends of elastic tog, and weave in ends.

Helpful Hint:

If you are a beginner and have difficulty understanding a pattern, then why not ask for someone's help? It's much better than being frustrated.

Words of Encouragement

Do you focus on your problems and wonder why they are not solved? My husband shares this approach in his "Yes You Can" Seminar — we tend to spend 90% of our time on the problem and 10% of our time on the solution. We become far more effective when we reverse that tendency and spend 10% of our time on the problem and 90% on solutions! 90% of the things we worry about never happen anyway, so it's better to spend more time coming up with a solution than worrying about the problem itself.

Skill Level — Beginner

SUPER BULKY
6
SUPER BULKY
Super Abultado

Finished size — 77" long x 2¼" wide

Spiral Scarf

This scarf is a fun, quick project — and you can watch it twist as you go! Make it with or without the contrasting trim.

Materials:

3 skeins (2.5 oz./70 g/ 57 yd.) yarn in lime/blue

2 skeins (2.5 oz/70 g/ 57 yd.) yarn in lime

Size P (15 mm), size N/13 (9 mm) and size H/8 (5 mm) hooks

Yarn needle

Used in this project: Lion Brand Bouclé in Lime/Blue and Lime

Gauge:

2 sc (with N hook) = approx. 1"

2 sc (with H hook) = approx. ⅝"

INSTRUCTIONS:

With 2 strands of A held tog and P hook, ch 110.

Row 1: Change to N hook. 4 sc in 2nd ch from hook; continue working 4 sc in each sc to end of row. End off.

Note: For a looser spiral, work 3 scs into each ch instead of 4. For a wider spiral, work 4 dcs instead of scs. Scarf will spiral by itself.

Lime Edging

With H hook, attach yarn to first sc on either end of scarf. Work 2 sc in each sc to end, working in top 2 lps only. End off.

Helpful Hint:
Use smaller yarn to make a spiral belt.

Words of Encouragement

When life seems to be spiraling out of control, seek God. Learning His ways will help you find purpose, and in finding purpose, you will find happiness and fulfillment. Things can turn around for you, even if sometimes it seems like an impossibility. If your watch breaks, you take it to a jewelry store to get it fixed, because they know more about fixing it than anyone else. If your life is broken, take it to God to get it fixed. He created you and is always there, willing to help. All you have to do is seek Him and ask for His guidance. He is there with open arms and will never turn you away. Look at His word as your owner's manual for life.

Skill Level — Advanced Beginner

BULKY
5
BULKY
Abultado

Finished size — 67" long x 3½" wide when hanging (8" wide when pulled open)

Popcorn Scarf

Do your own thing with this scarf and make a belt using smaller yarn and a smaller hook. Do you aspire to achieve your goals? Remember, "If you fail to plan, your plans will fail." Take action and make it happen!

Materials:

1 skein (3.5 oz/100 g/
129 yd.) bulky yarn
in garnet

Size J/10 (6 mm) hook

Yarn needle

*Used in this project:
Yarn Bee Islandic
Jewels in Garnet
(from Hobby Lobby)*

Gauge:

1 Popcorn St = ⅞"

10 chs = 3"

Special Stitch:

Popcorn St (pc): In
designated st, work 5
dc, take hook off yarn
lp and put hook into top
of ch 4. Then, working
in back of 5 dcs, place
hook through loose lp,
yo and pull through lp on
hook from the back.

INSTRUCTIONS:

Row 1: Ch 32, sc in second ch from
hook, * ch 10, work pc st in fourth
ch from hook, ch 3, sl st through lp
at base of pc (ch 3 is where you will
connect the next row with a sl st), ch
6, sl st in tenth free ch of foundation ch
below, and rep from * twice. End with
last sl st in last ch, turn — 3 pc sts.

Row 2: Ch 17, * pc in fourth ch from
hook, ch 3, sl st through lp at base of
pc, ch 6, sl st around ch 3 in back of
next pc (on prev row) ch 10, rep from
* twice, but do not ch 10 second time
around, turn — 3 pc sts.

Rows 3-25: Rep Row 2. End off.

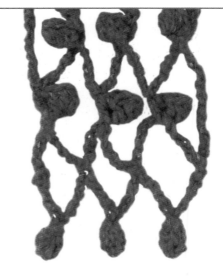

Finishing

On each ch-10 sp of foundation row:
Sl st in center ch of first ch 10 sp, ch
2, work pc in same sp, but do not ch
after pc st. End off. Rep on other 2
ch-10 sps.

Words of Encouragement

*Everything begins as a thought. The chair you are sitting in began as a thought. Your next
crochet project began as a thought. You have the ability to succeed with your ideas, but
first you need to set short-term and long-term goals. If you want to accomplish your
goal, do something every single day that will help you reach that goal, whether it requires
10 minutes or one hour. It could be just jotting down notes or saying something positive.
Persistence and patience go a long way. They will help you succeed in anything you do.*

Skill Level — Advanced Beginner

BULKY
5
BULKY
Abultado

Finished size — 58½", including tassels

Ribbon Scarf

This beautiful scarf is perfect for a dressy outfit, but it also looks fantastic with jeans. The ribbon with metallic threads is easy to work with, and the sparkle makes it special!

Materials:

1 hank (1.76 oz./50 g/ 66 yd.) metallic ribbon yarn in variegated fushia, green and rust

Size J/10 (6 mm) hook

Yarn needle

Sewing needle and matching thread

Used in this project: Sari Ribbon Yarn by Louisa Harding, color #10.

Gauge:

3 chains = 1"

2 dc = ⅝"

3 circles = 10"

INSTRUCTIONS:

Start with long center ch, then work in rnds.

Rnd 1: Ch 137, 1 sc in second ch from hook, * ch 4, sk 4 chs, 1 sc in next ch, rep from *. End with sc in last ch — 27 ch-4 lps.

At end of Row 1, work 4 sc in same sp where last sc was worked (called 4 sc group). Ch 4, continuing on other side of foundation ch. Work as follows: * sk 4 chs, sc in next ch, ch 4, rep from * to end of row. Work 4 sc in last ch same as other end (called ch 4 group).

Rnd 2: Continuing around other side, * ch 1, in ch-4 lp work (2 dc, ch 3, 2 dc, ch 3, 2 dc, ch 3, 2 dc- shell made) ch 1, sc in next ch 4 lp, rep from * across row. At end (after last sh), sc in first sc of 4 sc group, ch 4, sc in fourth sc of 4 sc group, cont around, ch 1, rep sh

patt as on other side. End with 1 sc in first sc on end (of 4 sc group), ch 4, sl st in fourth sc. End off. Weave in ends.

Tassel

Make 2 tassels 6" long: Wrap yarn around 6" piece of cardboard 10 times. Slip 12" piece of yarn under the yarn at the top of the cardboard, and tie a tight knot, leaving ends to attach tassel to scarf; remove from cardboard. Cut another 12" piece of yarn, wrap around top of tassel about ½" from top, and tie knot. Trim ends evenly. Weave remaining loose ends into center of tasel. Attach tassel to ch 4 on ends of scarf.

To weave ribbon through open sps on scarf: Cut 2 strands of ribbon 62" long. Weave through sps as in photo, leaving tail below ends of scarf. Attach ribbon to back bottom edge with sewing needle and thread.

Words of Encouragement

Do you dress up on the outside by making sure your hair, make-up, and clothes are just right, but on the inside you are full of bitterness, resentment, jealously and pride? Physical looks can create a good impression, but it's even more important to look beautiful on the inside with a good attitude and pure heart. What's on the inside will shine through!

Swarovski Crystals Ring

Sparkly genuine crystals make this quick and easy ring special — people will not even know that you made it! The metallic elastic thread stretches for adjustability.

One size fits all   *Skill Level — Beginner*

Materials:

Silver elastic thread

3 Swarovski crystal beads (any size)

US steel hook 8 (1.25 mm)

34-gauge wire

Sewing needle

INSTRUCTIONS:
Band:

Rnd 1: Ch 19, join with sl st to form a ring, ch 1, sc in each ch around, sl st to first sc. End off. Sew 3 crystal beads to top of ring with sewing needle and wire.

Words of Encouragement
Are you down on yourself and sometimes feel worthless? You are a unique individual and there's nobody on earth just like you. You were meant to sparkle. God made you special and He genuinely loves you more than you can imagine. He longs to have a relationship with you. The book of Psalms says, He "catches your tears in a jar" and you are the "apple of His eye!"

Multicolor Beaded Ring

Materials:

Silver elastic thread

12 glass beads in various colors (with holes large enough for elastic thread to go through)

30-34 gauge wire

US steel hook 8 (1.25 mm)

INSTRUCTIONS:

String beads onto elastic thread.

Row 1: Ch 2, sc in second ch, ch 1, turn – 1 sc.

Cont working 1 sc per row for 1¼", pull up first bead, ch tightly around it; rep with rem 10 beads, allowing them to bunch up, and sl st to first row. End off.

Note: If you want the beads stacked up, use wire and manipulate them to go where you want them. Secure end of wire by running it through chs and scs next to beads.

One size fits all

Skill Level — Beginner

Skill Level — Beginner

Finished size — Approx. 55½", without fringe

Confetti Scarf

Combining a small crochet thread and confetti carrying yarn may seem odd, but seeing the two lying next to each other inspired me to create this lovely scarf. The color combination is wonderful, and these two threads turned out to be very compatible.

Materials:

2 balls (1 oz./29 g each)
100% polyester confetti
yarn in lilac (A)

2 balls (150 yd.
each) 100% cotton
mercerized cotton
thread #3 in mint (B)

Size K/10.5
(6.5 mm) hook

Yarn needle

*Used in this project:
J&P Coats Royale
100% cotton thread
#3 in Sage Green (B)*

Gauge:

2 sc = ½"

7 sc rows = 2"

INSTRUCTIONS:

With two strands (A and B) held tog,
ch 13 loosely.

Row 1: Sc in second ch from hook
and in each ch across, ch 1, turn
— 12 sc.

Rows 2-194: Sc in each sc across,
ch 1, turn. End off — 12 sc.

Finishing

Cut 48 strands of confetti yarn 14"
long. Take 2 strands and fold in half;
attach folded end to end of scarf. Rep
with remaining strands, attaching 24
strands to each end of scarf.

Helpful Hint:

*Original patterns are pro-
tected by copyright, but
stitches or stitch patterns
can be used by anyone to
create an original design.
Buy a book that contains
numerous stitch patterns,
such as The Crochet Stitch
Bible. If you want to become
a designer, a book like this is
a valuable resource.*

Words of Encouragement

*Sometimes when people get married and discover their spouse actually has faults, they
wonder if they married the right person. They think they are not compatible. Remember
— problems are signposts to success. Differences, when met properly, become opportunities to grow and change. A good relationship comes from solving problems rather than
finding a situation where there are no problems. Try not to get discouraged when there is
conflict; anyone can learn to get along, if they are willing to work at it.*

Skill Level — Intermediate

MEDIUM
4
MOYEN
Medio

Fits girls' sizes 14-16 (16½" long) and women's xs (sm, med, lg, xlg, 1x and 2x)
Sm — 17½" long, med — 18" long, lg — 19" long, xlg, 1x and 2x — 19½" long

Tangerine Top

Make this top in bright, summery tangerine. Sometimes it's fun to
expand your horitzons and try colors that aren't your favorites. I'm
not crazy about orange, but I absolutely love this feminine top. Great
things can happen when you think outside the box!

Materials:

3 (4, 4, 5, 5, 6, 6) skeins
(3.5 oz./100 g/
178 yd.) 51% cotton
49% acrylic yarn in
light orange

Size G/6 (4 mm)
crochet hook

1 yd. ⅜"-wide ribbon

Yarn needle

Sewing needle and
matching thread

*Used in this project: TLC
Cotton Plus yarn in
Tangerine*

Gauge:

4 dc rows = 2"

5 dc = 1¼"

*Having the right gauge is
very important for this top.
If gauge does not match,
change to a larger hook.*

Special Stitch:

Work loose dcs.

Bobble St (bbl): Yo, insert
hook in st, pull through
2 lps (5 times) yo and
pull through all 6 lps on
hook — do not ch 1
after bbl st.

INSTRUCTIONS:

Back: Ch 62 (66, 68, 72, 74, 74, 74).

Row 1: Dc in fourth ch from hook and in each ch across. Ch 3, turn — 60 (64, 66, 70, 72, 72, 72) dc.

Note: Ch 3 will count as first dc throughout patt.

Row 2: Dc in blo of each st across row, ch 3, turn. Remember to always sk first dc that is attached to ch 3 — 60 (64, 66, 70, 72, 72, 72) dc.

Rows 2-24 (26, 28, 30, 32, 36, 38): Rep Row 2. End off.

Front

Rep Rows 1-24 (26, 28. 30, 32, 36, 38) same as back. Pm here to indicate front. With RS tog, sew side seams with yarn and yarn needle, leaving 18 (20, 22, 24, 26, 26, 26) dc unworked for armhole. Turn top RS out.

Attaching Front to Back at Shoulders

At armhole opening (on either side), attach yarn with sl st to top corner of back that is to rt of opening. Counting sl st as first ch, ch 13 (15, 17, 19, 21, 25, 27) attach with sl st to corner st on front piece to close armhole opening. End off — 13 (15, 17, 19, 21, 25, 27) chs. Rep on other side.

Top Edge

With RS out, attach yarn to corner at RS when back piece is facing you. This is the same sp where you attached sl st for chs.

Rnd 1: At top neck edge, working on ends of dc rows, work 2scstog across back. (To work 2sctog, insert hook around body of dc at end of first dc row, yo and pull lp through, leaving 2 lps on hook. Insert hook in st before next dc row, yo and pull up lp, yo and pull through all 3 lps on hook.) You are working a 2sctog with both sts worked over 1 row. The first sc is worked around post of the dc and the second sc is worked at the end of the same dc — before next dc. (See Diagram C.) Cont across top edge working 2sctog, until you get to corner — 24 (26, 28, 30, 32, 36, 38) sc total. After working sc in side of last dc, work 1 sc in corner st, work 13 (15, 17, 19, 21, 25, 27) sc in chs across shoulder, sl st to next corner.

Diagram C

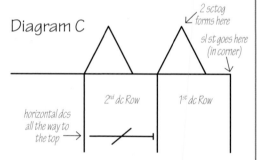

Next Step: Work 24 (26, 28, 30, 32, 36, 38) sc across front with 2sctog same as on back, work 13 (15, 17, 19, 21, 25, 27) sc in next 13 (15, 17, 19, 21, 25, 27) sc across shoulder, attach to first sl st in corner.

Rnd 2 (Rnd where ribbon will be woven through): Ch 3, dc in each of next 24 (26, 28, 30, 32, 36, 38) sc, dc in corner st — 26 (28, 30, 32, 34, 38, 40) total dc across back.

Words of Encouragement

*Look for good in others. When I was growing up, my mother told me that you can always
find something good to say about anyone — so focus on the good in others, not the bad.
You will reap what you sow, and others will be more likely to find the good in you. It's not
always natural to be positive, but with practice you can learn to change any negative patterns that you learned while growing up.*

Next Step: Work sc in same st as last dc worked (corner st). Bbl will be on WS, but when row is finished, carefully push each one to RS with finger. * Work bobble (see special st) in next sc, sc in next st, rep from * 5 (6, 7, 8, 9, 11, 12) times, sc in corner st — 6 (7, 8, 9, 10, 12, 13) bbl sts.

Next Step: Work front same as back — 26 (28, 30, 32, 34, 38, 40) dc.

Note: first and last dc will be worked in corner sts on each end of front and back.

Next Step: Work sc in same st as last dc, work bbl sts across ch 13 (15, 17, 19, 21, 25, 27) same as before, and sl st to top of ch 3 at beg of rnd. End off.

Remainder of Shoulder
Work on free lps of chain.

Row 2 of shoulder/sleeve: Turn top inside-out with neck edge closest to you. On either shoulder, attach yarn to RS of sleeve opening at underside of bbl row. Attach with sl st to third dc as in Diagram D. Sc to free lp of first ch on unworked edge of ch 13 (15, 17, 19, 21, 25, 27). * Bbl in next ch, sc in next ch, rep from * 5 (6, 7, 8, 9, 11, 12) times, sl st to third and fourth dc on armhole opening, ch 1, and turn — 6 (7, 8, 9, 10, 12, 13) bbls.

Row 3: Work 13 (15, 17, 19, 21, 25, 27) sc across row, attach with sl st to fourth and fifth dc on armhole opening, ch 1, and turn.

Row 4: Working into sc instead of chs, work 6 (7, 8, 9, 10, 12, 13) bbls with sc between each as in Row 2. Attach to fourth and fifth dc, ch 1, turn.

Row 5: Work 13 (15, 17, 19, 21, 25, 27) sc across, attach to sixth and seventh dc, ch 1, turn.

Row 6: Rep Row 4, attaching to sixth and seventh dc on side edge, ch 1, turn.

Row 7: Rep Row 5, attaching to eighth and ninth dc, ch 1, turn.

Row 8: Rep Row 4, attaching to eighth and ninth dc, ch 1, turn.

Row 9: Rep Row 5, attaching to tenth and eleventh dc, ch 1, turn.

Row 10: Rep Row 4, attaching to tenth and eleventh dc, ch 1, turn.

Row 11: Work 13 (15, 17, 19, 21, 25, 27) sc across, attaching to tenth dc. End off.

Work other shoulder in same manner.

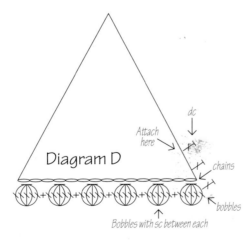

Diagram D

Attach here

dc

chains

bobbles

Bobbles with sc between each

Bobble Edging

Rnd 1: At bottom edge, attach yarn to seam on either side. Sc in same sp, * sc around post of next horizontal dc, sc in sp before next dc row, and rep from * around. Sl st to first sc.

Rnd 2: Ch 1, sc in same sp, * bbl in next sc, sc in next sc, rep from *. End with sl st in first sc. End off.

Finishing

If needed, adjust armhole opening by sewing up more sts at side seam, or work scs around entire armhole opening. For larger armhole opening, take out some sts. Weave in ends.

Cut ends of ribbon at a slant. Starting at center space on dc row of top front, weave ribbon through all dc around, allowing ribbon to lie loose underneath bbl row. Tack loose ribbon to underside of bbl row with needle and thread.

Finished size — 2¾" x 2¾", without handles

Skill Level — Advanced Beginner

Purse Keychain

This darling little purse keychain would be a great quick gift idea for friends — and they will remember you each time they pick up their keys. This nylon cord comes in many solid and variegated colors.

Materials:

1 spool (7 oz./200 g) nylon cord in olive green (1 spool makes 4 purse keychains)

Size E/4 (3.5 mm) hook

⅓" decorative button for tab

1 key ring

1 snap for closure

Yarn needle

Used in this project: Hilos 100% nylon cord #18 in Olive (see resources, pg. 125). Substitute J&P Coats Crochet Nylon cord or any #2 yarn wt.

Gauge:

5 sc = 1⅛"

5 sc rows= 1"

Helpful Hint:

To remember where you are on a pattern, put the pattern in a plastic sleeve and use a highlighter to mark each step as you have worked it. That way, you will not lose your place. Just wipe the plastic clean when you are finished.

INSTRUCTIONS:

Rnd 1: Ch 11, sc in second ch from hook and in each ch across (10 sc), work 2 more sc in last sc, cont around, work scs in each free ch on other side, 2 more sc in last ch, join to first sc — 24 sc.

Rnd 2: Ch 1, inc 3 sc on each end, sc in each sc around. End off — 30 sc. (Body is worked separately and attached later.)

Body of Purse
Rnd 1: Ch 30, join with sl st to form a ring, ch 1, sc in same sp as sl st and in each ch around. Join to first sc — 30 sc.

Rnds 2-12: Ch 1, sc in same sp and in each sc around. End off — 30 sc.

Tab
Row 1: Pm at center st on back, 3 rows down from top edge. Attach cord to 1 st over at rt of center st, ch 1, sc in same st, sc in next 2 sts, ch 1, turn — 3 sc.

Rows 2-10: Sc in each sc, ch 1, turn — 3 sc.

Row 11: 2sctog in first 2 sc (see pg. 9 for 1 dec), sc in next sc — 2 sc.

Row 12: 2sctog in rem 2 sc. End off — 1 sc. Sew button to tab.

Handles
Make 2.

Cut 2 strands of cord 72" each. Fold 1 cord in half, doubling the cord for each handlem Make slipknot, leaving a 3" tail. Tightly ch 18. End off.

Attach handles with front of purse facing you.

From inside, pull loose ends of handle through st with hook (3 sts down from top edge and 3 sts over from tab). Pull ends to inside, tying a knot close to st; rep on other end. Rep to attach handle to back side.

Attaching Bottom to Purse Body
Place bottom piece on end of purse, attaching each short end with a small piece of cord, holding it in place. Cut a 36" piece of cord. With yarn needle and 1 strand of cord, attach bottom to purse (easing in to fit), stitching on outside edges.

Key Ring
With front facing you, on left inside of purse, attach cord to center st on second row from top, ch 2, sl st cord to ring, 2 sc on ring, turn and sl st in each ch to end, sl st to st at left of sp where cord was attached at beg. End off.

One size fits most

Skill Level — Intermediate

SUPER BULKY
6
SUPER BULKY
Super Abultado

Newsboy Cap

This cute and fashionable hat may look difficult to the beginner, but the pattern is constructed in a way that is very easy to follow. Wear it as you see in the photo, or flatten the top toward the brim for a Gatsby-style hat.

Materials:

- 3 skeins (2 oz./70 g/ 57 yd. each) yarn in hot pink
- Size J/10 (6 mm), H/8 (5 mm) and F/5 (3.75 mm) hooks
- Yarn needle

Used in this project: Lion Brand Bouclé yarn in Rose. Substitute two strands med. worsted-wt. yarn

Gauge:

- Finished hat should measure approx. 11" in diameter when lying flat
- 3 dc = approx. 1¼"
- 2 dc rows = approx. 2"

INSTRUCTIONS:

With J hook, ch 4, sl st in first ch to form ring.

Rnd 1: Ch 4 (counts as first dc, ch 1) 5 times, 1 dc into ring, sl st in third ch of ch 4 — 12 dc, 6 ch-1 sps.

Rnd 2: Sl st in next ch, ch 4, 1 dc in same ch sp, * dc in each of 2 dc, (dc, ch 1, dc) in ch 1 sp; rep from * 4 more times, dc in next 2 dc, join — 24 dc and 6 ch 1 sps (4 dc between ch 1 sps).

Rnd 3: Sl st in next ch, ch 4, 1 dc in same ch sp, * dc in each of next 4 dc, (dc, ch 1, dc) in ch 1 sp; rep from * 4 more times, dc in next 4 dc, join — 36 dc (6 dc between ch 1 sps).

Rnd 4: Rep Rnd 3, working 8 dc between ch-1 sps — 48 dc.

Rnd 5: Rep Rnd 3, working 10 dc between ch-1 sps — 60 dc.

Rnd 6: Rep Rnd 3, working 12 dc between ch-1 sps —72 dc.

Rnd 7: Dec rnd (will have 10 dc between sps). Sl st over to first dc, ch 3 (counts as first dc), 2dctog in next 2 dc (see pg. 9 to dec). Dc in each of next 7 dc, 2dctog in next 2 dc, * ch 1, 2dctog in next 2 dc, dc in each of next 8 dc, 2dctog in next 2 dc; rep from * 4 more times. End with ch 1, join — 60 dc (10 dc between ch 1 sps).

Rnd 8: Work even with 10 dc between ch 1 sps — 60 dc.

Rnd 9: Dec rnd.

Work this rnd with 8 dc between ch 1 sps, as in Rnd 7 — 48 dc.

Band

Rnd 10: Change to size H hook. Ch 1, sc in same sp and in each dc around, skipping ch 1 sps, join — 48 sc.

Rnd 11: Ch 1, sc in same sp and in each sc around, join. End off.

Top Stitching for Ridge on Top

With 2 strands and H hook, work ridges in the ch 1 sps (between pie shapes) as follows: With RS of hat facing, holding yarn on inside of hat, insert hook into circle at top center of hat, and sl st yarn into any ch 1 sp on first rnd. These sl sts need to be long and loose (approx. 1") to keep from pulling up the hat and distorting it. Cont to make loose sl sts in ch 1 sps in Rnds 2-9, forming a decorative ridge. This will fill in the holes and round off the corners. After sl stitching in last ch-1 sp (Rnd 9), sl st into the sc on Rnd 10. End off.

Brim

Pm in sc on last rnd of band below any sl st ridge. This will designate middle of brim. Brim rows will not be turned. End off each row (all rows facing RS). Take H hook and single strand of yarn, and with RS of Rnd 11 (hat band) facing, join yarn with sl st in seventh st to rt of marker.

Row 1: Ch 1, sc in same sp as joining, sc in next 13 sts. End off — 14 sts.

Row 2: With RS facing, join yarn in first st to the rt of Row 1, 1 sc in each of next 3 sts, 2 sc in next st (inc made) 1 sc in each of next 6 sts, 2 sc in next st (inc) 1 sc in each of last 3 sts. End off —16 sc.

Row 3: With RS facing you, join yarn in band 2 sts over from beg of brim, 1 sc in each of these 2 sts, 1 sc in each of next 4 sts of brim, 2 sc in next st, 1 sc in each of next 6 sts, 2 sc in next st, 1 sc in each of last 4 sts of brim, 1 sc in each of next 2 sts in band. End off — 22 sts.

Rows 4-5: Cont working 2 more sts of band (on each side) and 2 more sts (incs) above inc of prev row (6 inc on each row), Row 4 (28 sts), Row 5 (34 sts). Mark incs. End off.

Row 6: From left side, count over (toward the middle) to seventh st on brim. Pm in seventh st. From rt, count over to fourth sc, attach yarn with sl st (do not sc in same sp as sl st), 1 sc in each of next 3 sc, 2 sc in next sc, sc in each st until you get to marker (st 7). 2 sc in this st (inc), 1 sc in each of next 3 sc, sl st in next sc. End off.

Button

With F hook, ch 3, sl st in third ch to form ring. Ch 1, 12 sc in ring, join. End off. Sew button to top of hat. Weave in ends.

Optional: If you want a wider band, work a sc row in back of hat from one end of Rnd 5 to the other end.

The finished hat measures 11" when lying flat.

Finished size — all sizes, 2¼" wide x desired length

Skill Level — Advanced Beginner

FINE
2
FIN
Fino

Lace Belt

This stylish, original belt can be worn many ways, and it would look great in any color, with or without the picot edging. Wear it as a hip belt or on the waist — either way, you'll look great!

INSTRUCTIONS:

Row 1: With F hook, ch 10, sc in second ch from hook, and in each ch, ch 3 (counts as first dc of Row 2), turn — 9 sc.

Row 2: 1 dc in the second sc, * ch 1, 1 dc in same sc (V-st made), sk 2 sc, dc in next sc; rep from * twice. End with dc in last sc, ch 3, turn — 3 dc V-sts + 1 dc on each end.

Row 3: Work 3-dc cl in the ch-1 sp of V-st (see special st), * ch 2, work 3 dc cl in next ch 1 sp. Rep from *. End with dc in top of tch, ch 1, turn — 3 dc cls + 1 dc on each end.

Row 4: Sc in first dc, in dc clusters and in every ch across row, ch 1, turn — 9 sc.

Row 5: Sc across row, ch 3, turn — 9 sc.

Rep Rows 2-5 (21) times or until desired length, ending with Row 3. Work last 2 sc rows at end of belt as follows:

Row 1: Sc dec over first 2 sts, sc in next 5 sc, 2sctog over last 2 sts — 7 sc (see pg. 9).

Row 2: Sc dec over first 2 sts, sc in next 3 sc, sc dec over next 2 sts. End off — 5 sc.

Attaching Buckle

On opp end of belt, fold 1¾" to back, placing buckle inside at fold. If you have a metal belt lp (as in photo), place this under fold also. Sew folded piece to back side of belt with needle and thread.

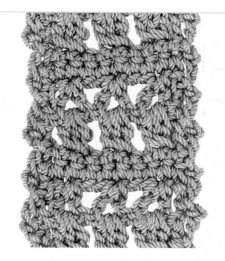

Picot Edging

Work on outside edge of belt. With RS of belt facing and D hook, attach cord with sl st to side of belt next to buckle, * (ch 3, sl st in second ch from hook — p made), sk approx. ½", sl st to side edge; rep from * around entire belt edge, ending at st right before buckle. Weave in ends.

Materials:

1 spool (7 oz./200 g) nylon cord in taupe

Size F/5 (3.75 mm) and size D/3 (3.25 mm) hooks

1 belt buckle, 2½" wide

Sewing needle and thread to match belt

Used in this project: Hilos #18, 100% nylon cord, see resources, pg. 125. Substitute J&P Coats Crochet Nylon Cord or any sport-wt. yarn.

Gauge:

9 sc = 1⅞"

2 V-st = 1¼"

(2) 3 dc cluster = ½"

Special Stitch:

V-Stitch: (Dc, ch 1, dc) in same st.

3-dc Cluster Stitch (cl): (Yo, insert hook in ch-1 sp, yo and pull up lp, yo and pull through 2 lps) 3 times. Yo and pull through all 4 lps on hook.

Picot Stitch (p): Ch 3, sl st in second ch from hook.

Words of Encouragement

We are all genuine original human beings! But sometimes we have character flaws or patterns of behavior in our lives that prevent us from being who we want to be. We all know that nobody is perfect, but the key is to keep trying. Something that helped me actually take steps to change was making notes of I Cor. 13 (the love chapter), such as "Mary Jane is kind, Mary Jane is patient, etc." At first I didn't believe it, but the more I saw that in my mind, the more I started to think it could really happen. I'm certainly not perfect, and never will be, but visualizing what I want to be really helps.

Helpful Hint:

If you have trouble finding a belt buckle, visit a thrift store!

Skill Level — Intermediate

BULKY
5
BULKY
Abultado

Fits sizes med-lg (xlg)

Sari Silk Bolero

Try different yarns, such as sari silk yarn made from remnants of saris in the factories of Nepal. You will not only be helping the women of Nepal when you buy this yarn, but you will be surprised and delighted at what you can create with it. It's like painting your own unique canvas of colorful images!

INSTRUCTIONS:
Make 2.

Beg at lower edge of sleeve, ch 25 (28). Join to first ch to form a ring.

Rnd 1: Ch 3 (always counts as first dc), dc in bottom of ch 3 (making this your first inc), dc in next ch and in each ch across, join to top of ch 3 with sl st — 26 (29) dc.

Rnd 2: (From here on out, each round will be increased, but since sari silk yarn is inconsistent in size/wt, you may only need to inc every other row for sari yarn and every row for worsted-wt. yarn). Ch 3, dc in same sp as join-ing (inc made) dc in each dc around, join to top of ch 3 with sl st, now and throughout pattern — 27 (30) dc.

Rnds 3-18: Rep Rnd 2, increasing 1 dc at beg of each rnd. Rnd 18 should have 43 (46) dc. Pm at middle st of Rnd 18.

Rnd 19: Ch 3, dc in same sp (inc) dc in each rem st around, working 2 dc (inc) in st where marker was placed. Join — 2 inc on Rnd — 45 (48) dc. Pm in middle st.

Rnd 20: Rep Rnd 19, 2 inc = 47 (50) dc.

Rnd 21: Rep Rnd 19, 2 inc = 49 (52) dc.

Rnd 22: Rep Rnd 19, 2 inc = 51 (54) dc.

Rnd 23: Ch 3, dc in same sp, dc in each of next 4 dc, * 2 dc in next dc, dc in each of next 4 dc; rep from * around. End with 1 dc in each of last 5 (3) dc, 10 (11) inc = 61 (65) dc.

Rnd 24: Rep Rnd 19, pm in middle st before beginning, 2 inc — 63 (67) dc.

Rnd 25: Rep Rnd 23, end with dc in each of last 2 (1) dc —13 (14) inc = 76 (81) dc.

Rnd 26: Ch 3, dc in same st, * dc in each of next 5 dc, 2 dc in next dc; rep from * around. End with dc in each of last 3 (2) dc — 13 (14) inc = 89 (95) dc.

Rnd 27: Rep Rnd 19 — 2 inc = 91 (97) dc.

Rnd 28: Rep Rnd 26, but instead of 5 dc between each inc, work 6 dc be-tween each inc. End with dc in last 6 (4) dc — 13 (14) inc = 104 (111) dc.

Rnd 29: Rep Rnd 26 with 6 dc between. End with dc in last 5 (5) dc —15 (15) inc = 119 (126) dc.

Start Shoulder Shaping
Rnd 30: Rep Rnd 19 — 2 inc = 121 (130) dc.

Rnd 31: Rep Rnd 19 — 2 inc = 123 (132) dc.

Rnd 32: Rep rnd 19 — 2 inc = 125 (134) dc.

Materials:
4 hanks (200 g/160 yd.) sari silk yarn (multicolor)
Size J/10 (6 mm) hook
1 wooden toggle button
Yarn needle
Markers
Sewing needle and matching thread

Gauge:
Gauge is extremely important with this yarn.
6 dc = 2"
6 dc rows = 3¾"

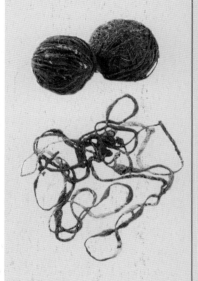

Helpful Hint:
Since sari yarn is incon-sistent in color and size in each skein, you may need to alternate skeins with every row. If using sari silk yarn, it is imperative to count every row due to the inconsistent nature of the yarn. You need patience to work with this material.

Words of Encouragement
The human mind is like a canvas. What are you painting on the canvas of other people's minds? I'll never forget this statement: "People will live up to whatever they think the most important person in their life thinks of them." If you call them bad or lazy, then that's what they'll tend to become. A 300-lb. girl in her 20s once told me that when she was little, her dad constantly called her "fat girl." He thought that would make her want to eat less, but with tears in her eyes, she told me that it made her want to eat more. Without realizing it, he made things worse with the image he painted on the canvas of her mind. But it's never too late — start painting positive images and see what kind of results you get!

Rnd 33: Rep Rnd 19 — 2 inc = 127 (136) dc.

Rnd 34: Rep Rnd 19 — 2 inc = 129 (138) dc. End off. Pm at bottom side seam, and pm at middle st on row, which will be at the shoulder.

(For size xlg only: Add additional rows as needed; inc every other row)

Back Seam

Try both pieces on and if they do not reach in back, add more rows, adding only enough incs to make it fit snugly around shoulders. The piece can be a little wavy, but that's normal. Blocking will help to smooth it out. Lay the two pieces side by side on a table (or try the pieces on and have someone help you). Pm in back where you want seam to begin and end. You should have an inverted V shape at the bottom center in back. Sewing up too many sts will cause the sides and front not to fit — approx. 40 sts. Sew up back seam with yarn and yarn needle.

Finishing — Front Button Closure

With sewing needle and thread, sew wooden button at left front, where desired. Attach yarn to other side of bolero front with sl st, at place that corresponds to button. Ch 5, turn and sl st in next st (from where attached) to form lp. End off, and weave in all loose ends. This bolero will need to be blocked.

Note: With sari silk yarn, no two skeins are alike. Sometimes it has the consistency of thread, worsted-weight, and bulky yarn all in one skein. Since there are inconsistencies, you may need to add one or more rounds to one sleeve in order to match the other.

Wood and Metal Necklace

You can crochet several of these necklaces for friends to put smiles on their faces. Make them in different colors and lengths, and everyone will have a unique gift!

One size fits most   *Skill Level — Beginner*

Materials:

6 ft. (approx.) waxed jute string. Substitute hemp or crochet thread

3 round ¾" wood beads

4 round/flat ½" metal copper-colored beads

Size D/3 (3.25 mm) hook (or smaller)

Gauge:

3 chs = ¾"

INSTRUCTIONS:

With needle, string beads onto jute in order that they will be placed onto necklace. Make slipknot, leaving 10" tail at beg. Ch 13, pull up smaller metal bead and ch 1 around it. * Ch 3, pull up larger wooden bead and ch 1 around it; rep from *, alternating beads, making sure larger bead is in center. After you have strung all 7 beads, ch 13. End off, leaving a 10" tail, so necklace can be tied in back of neck. Tie knot in each end of necklace.

Words of Encouragement

Do you smile much? Do other people smile at you? The best way to get a smile is to give one. A simple smile with genuine interest in others can brighten a room. You don't want to be the kind of person who brightens a room by leaving it!

One size fits most

MEDIUM
4
MOYEN
Medio

Granny Squares Braided Cap

Granny squares are still popular, so why not make this 60s-inspired cap with funky braids? If you get cold, just wrap the braids around to hug your neck and wear as a scarf! The cap will look cute with either short or long braids.

INSTRUCTIONS:
Granny Square 1
Puff st flower square— make 4.

With color B and G hook, ch 4, sl st to form ring.

Rnd 1: Puff st in ring, ch 3 (4 times), end with ch 3, sl st to top of first puff st. End off — 4 puff sts.

Rnd 2: With A, attach to any ch 3 corner sp, ch 3 (counts as first dc) in same sp work (2 dc, ch 3, 3 dc) * ch 1, in next ch 3 corner sp work (3 dc, ch 3, 3 dc) rep from * 2 more times, ch 1, sl st to third ch of ch 3. End off — 24 dc.

Granny Square 2
Make 4.

With MC ch 5, sl st to first ch to form ring.

Rnd 1: Ch 1, 3 sc in ring, ch 2, * 3 sc in ring, ch 2; rep from * 2 times, sl st to top of ch 1. End off.

Rnd 2: With B attach in any ch 2 sp, ch 1, in same sp work (3 hdc, ch 2, 3 hdc), * ch 1, in next ch 2 corner sp, work (3 hdc, ch 2, 3 hdc); rep from * 2 more times, ch 1, sl st to ch 1. End off.

Rnd 3: Attach A in any ch-2 corner sp, ch 3, in same sp work (1 hdc, ch 2, 2 hdc). * 3 hdc in next ch-1 sp, (2 hdc, ch 2, 2 hdc) in next ch-2 corner sp; rep from * 2 more times. 3 hdc in last ch-1 sp, sl st to ch 2. End off.

Sew squares tog, alternating Granny 1 and Granny 2, with yarn and yarn needle. With RS tog, sew short ends.

Cap
With MC and I hook, ch 4. Join with sl st to form ring.

Rnd 1: Ch 3, 2 dc in ring, ch 1, * (3 dc in ring, ch 1); rep from * 3 times, sl st to top of ch 3 — 5 sets of 3 dc.

Rnd 2: Sl st over to ch-1 sp, (ch 3, 2 dc, ch 1, 3 dc) in same sp, ch 1, (3 dc, ch 1, 3 dc in next ch 1 sp, ch 1) around, join — 30 dc.

Rnd 3: Sl st over to ch-1 sp, (ch 3, 2dc, ch 1, 3 dc) in same sp, ch 1, 3 dc in next ch 1 sp, ch 1. * (3 dc, ch 1, 3 dc) in next ch-1 sp, ch 1, 3 dc in next ch sp, ch 1; rep from * around, join — 45 dc.

Rnd 4: sl st over to ch-1 sp (ch 3, 2 dc) in same sp, ch 1, (3 dc in next ch-1 sp, ch 1) around, join — 45 dc.

Materials:
- 2 skeins (3 oz./85 g/ 147 yd. each) yarn in brown (MC)
- 1 skein (3 oz./113 g/ 190 yd.) yarn in green (A)
- 1 skein (3.5 oz./100 g/ 190 yd.) yarn in persimmon (B)
- Size G/6 (4 mm) and I/9 (5.5 mm) hooks
- Yarn needle

Used in this project: Lion Brand Wool-Ease in Mink Brown, Brown Sheep Lamb's Pride worsted wool in Kiwi and Red Heart Symphony in Persimmon.

Gauge:
- Each square = 2¼"-2½" (with G hook)
- 3 dc = ¾" (with I hook)

Special Stitch:
Puff Stitch: To make 4 dc puff st, ch 3, yo, insert hook into ring and pull up about ½" (4 times). With 9 lps on hook, yo and pull through all lps.

Words of Encouragement
You can never hug your kids too much, and they will never get tired of hearing that you love them. But do you know what will make your kids feel more loved and secure than anything else on this earth? I've heard it said by experts that what makes your children feel secure is knowing that their parents love each other. So if you spend more time with the kids and neglect your spouse, you are really hurting them in the long run. Make them feel more secure by giving your spouse extra attention. Maybe you can even plan a weekly "date." I know from experience that your kids will love it!

Helpful Hint:
If you prefer, make one large braid on each side instead of three!

Rnds 5-9: 3 dc in each ch-1 sp around with ch 1 between each set — 15 sets of 3-dc (45 dc on each rnd). With RS tog, sew granny square tube to edge of hat with yarn and yarn needle.

Edging

With G hook and A, sc in each st around. End off. Weave in ends.

Braids

Make 6 with MC.

1 braid: Cut 15 strands of yarn, 3 yds each. Fold the 15 strands, making it 30. Tie a piece of yarn at fold to secure. Separate the 30 strands into 3 groups of 10, and make a braid. Leaving about 6" of loose ends, place rubber band around braid. Wrap with yarn to cover.

With yarn, tie 3 braids tog at fold. On WS of cap, weave loose ends of yarn through granny square and tie to secure. Sew braids to cap on WS with needle and thread. Rep on other side.

Skill Level — Beginner

BULKY
5
BULKY
Abultado

Finished size — 7½" long, fits size sm (med, lg, xlg)

Ruffled Wrist Warmers

Wear these warm, fuzzy wrist warmers on a cold winter day, or make a fashion statement with a ruffled, feminine look. Your friends will be begging you for their own!

Materials:

1 skein (3.5 oz./ 100 g/310 yd.) fuzzy yarn in brown

Size J/10 (6 mm) hook

Yarn needle

Used in this project: Red Heart Symphony yarn in Earth Brown

Gauge:

2 dc = ¾"

2 dc rows = 1¾"

INSTRUCTIONS:

Make 2.

Row 1: With 2 strands of yarn, ch 19 (21, 23, 25), dc in fourth ch from hook and in each ch across, ch 3, turn — 17 (19, 21, 23) dc.

Row 2: Counting ch 3 as first dc, dc in each dc across, ch 3, turn — 17 (19, 21, 23) dc.

Rows 3-7: Rep Row 2. End off.

With RS tog, sew tog short sides with yarn and yarn needle. End off. Turn RS out.

Ruffle

Mark beg of each rnd.

Rnd 1: Attach yarn to any dc on either end, * ch 3, sk next dc, sl st in next dc, rep from * around, end with sl st to top of first ch-3 sp — 9 (10, 11, 12) ch-3 lps.

Rnd 2: * Ch 4, sc in next ch-3 lp, rep from * around; end with ch 4, sc in first ch-4 sp — 9 (10, 11, 12) ch-4 sps.

Rnd 3: * Ch 5, sc in next ch-4 sp, rep from * around, join. End off — 9 (10, 11, 12) ch-5 sps.

Rep Rnds 1-3 on other end.

Words of Encouragement

How easily do you get your feathers ruffled? It used to really bother me if someone broke a glass or spilled something on the carpet, because I thought people should be more careful. A long time ago, something happened that changed my priorities forever. A friend who had three little boys told me she wasn't comfortable bringing them over to be around all my "pretty little things." I said, "They haven't ever broken anything, and even if they ever did, I've decided that people are more important than things! I care more about you and your boys than I care about my things." I'm still not perfect at this, but I have tried to go by that philosophy for several years now, and I'm much happier.

Finished size — Adult (5½" x 83"), Child (3" x 52")

FINE
2
FIN
Fino

SUPER BULKY
6
SUPER BULKY
Super Abultado

Mother-Daughter Snowball Scarves

This scarf sparkles like new-fallen snow! Show off your precious little angel as you both wear look-alike accessories. Making these scarves would be a great way to start your holiday season — and you'll both feel warm and snuggly!

Materials:

4 skeins (3.5 oz./100 g/ 108 yd. each) yarn in white (2⅓ skeins for adult, 1⅓ skeins for child)

1 ball (3.52 oz./100 g/ 218 yd.) crochet cotton thread #5 in blue

Size N/15 (10 mm) and size B/1 (2.25 mm) hooks

Yarn needle

Sewing needle and matching thread

Used in this project: Yarn Bee Airy Yarn (from Hobby Lobby) in white, Sinfonia cotton yarn (see resources pg. 125) in blue. Substitute any #2 sportweight yarn.

Gauge:

3 sc and 3 sc rows = 1¾"

Pompoms = 2½" diameter (adult), 2" diameter

Snowflakes = 4" (adult), 2" (child)

Special Stitch:

Picot (p): Ch 3, sl st in first sc.

INSTRUCTIONS:

Adult Scarf

Row 1: With N hook, ch 10, sk first ch, * sc in next ch and each ch across, ch 1, turn — 9 sc.

Rows 2-116: Rep Row 1 from * into scs — 9 sc.

Pompoms

Make 6 (lg) 2½" pps for adult scarf and 4 (sm) 2" pps for child's scarf (use plain white yarn that will not break to tie center of pps).

Cut a piece of cardboard (1" for lg pps and ¾" for small pps). Wind yarn around the cardboard 105 times. Slip lps off the cardboard. Cut a 12" piece of yarn and slip it through the lps. Securely tie tog so the yarn will not come loose. Cut the lps on the untied end and fluff out the pp. Trim evenly to desired size.

Child's Scarf

Row 1: Ch 6, sk first ch, * sc in next ch and each ch across, ch 1, turn — 5 sc.

Rows 2-88: Rep Row 1 from * into scs.

Make 2 small pps. Gather short end of scarf and attach 1 pp; rep on other end.

Large Snowflake
Make 2.

Rnd 1: With B hook, ch 4, sl st to form a ring, ch 1, 6 sc in ring, sl st to first sc — 6 sc.

Rnd 2: * Ch 3, sl st in first sc (p made) sl st in next sc, rep from * around, sl st in first sc — 6 p.

Rnd 3: * Ch 8, sl st in third ch from hook (p) ch 5, sl st between next 2 p from prev rnd, rep from * around, sl st to first sl st — 6 pointed chs.

Rnd 4: * Ch 6, sl st in third ch (first p) ch 5, sl st in third ch (second p) ch 3, sl st in third ch (top p) sl st to center of second p (on opp side of stem) ch 3, sl st in third ch, sl st to second p again, sl st in next 2 chs, sl st to first p, ch 3, sl st in third ch, sl st in center of first p again, sl st in next 3 chs, sl st to base of stem, ch 1, sl st loosely in back of snowflake over to sp between next 2 pointed chs, being careful not to pull too tight. Ch 1, rep from * around, sl st to first sl st. End off — 6 stems.

Sew to ends of scarf with white thread and sewing needle.

Small Snowflake
Make 2.

With B hook, ch 4. Sl st to first ch to form a ring.

Rnd 1: (Ch 4, sl st in second ch, ch 2, sl st in ring) 6 times — 6 pointed ch lps.

Rnd 2: * Ch 6, sl st in third ch. End off. Attach yarn to sp between next 2 points and rep from * 5 times. Sew to ends of scarf.

To Attach Pompoms

Attach yarn to bottom rt corner of scarf, (ch 9, attach to 1 pp, ch 9, sk 1½", attach to edge of short end of scarf) 3 times. End with sl st to next corner. Rep on other end. For child's scarf, sew 2 pompoms to each end.

Words of Encouragement

Children are very precious. When people say, "Children are to be seen and not heard," it really bothers me. I've even heard of parents making their kids sit on the couch and not move a muscle when they go to visit someone. If children are not disciplined, they will not learn to be self-disciplined; but some people are just too hard on their children. Let kids be kids, with appropriate guidance and discipline, because they are little human beings with feelings just like you and me. My grandmother told me that God is allowing you to borrow them, so please take care of their physical needs and their fragile little spirits as well.

Skill Level — Advanced Beginner

MEDIUM
4
MOYEN
Medio

or

SUPER BULKY
6
SUPER BULKY
Super Abultado

Fits womens' sizes: x-sm, sm, med, lg (can also be made to fit little girls' sizes 4-6)

Fishnet Sweater

This unique sweater has an openweave stitch pattern and is full of holes. Since it's mainly for looks, you'll want to wear a long-sleeved top underneath! If you use a smaller cotton yarn, your little girl can wear it in warmer weather — or try using a P hook for plus-size!

Materials:

(Adult) 3 balls (2.5 oz./ 70 g/57 yd. each) bouclé yarn in variegated pink and purple

(Child) 2 hanks (1.75 oz./ 50 g/82 yd. each) yarn in cream

(Adult) Size K/10.5 (6.5 mm) hook (or size needed to obtain gauge)

(Child) Size H/8 (5 mm) hook (or size needed to obtain gauge

Used in this project:
(Adult) Lion Brand Bouclé yarn in Wild Berries.
(Child) Lion Organic Cotton in Vanilla

Gauge:

3 dtr sts with 2 ch-6 spaces in between = 6"

2 dtr rows = approx. 4½"

1 ch-6 space = approx. 2½"

1 ch-5 sp = approx. 2"

Special Stitch:

Double Treble (dtr) (sometimes called quadruple st): Yo 3 times, insert hook into st, draw up lp (5 lps on hook), yo and draw through two lps 4 times.

Chain 11 = dtr + ch 6 throughout

Helpful Hint:

If you use a smaller yarn and smaller hook, it will fit a small child. Try using a size P hook for plus sizes, etc. This is a really quick project!

INSTRUCTIONS:

This sweater begins at neck and is worked in rnds. Two rnds will be worked before skipping sp for armhole.

With K hook (H hook for child's size), ch 81, being careful not to twist ch. Join to first ch with sl st to form ring.

Rnd 1: Ch 11, sk 4 chs, 1 dtr into next ch, * ch 5, dtr in next ch, Rep from * around. End with ch 5 and sl st into fifth ch of ch-11 — 16 ch-5 sps.

Rnd 2: Ch 11 (counts as dtr + ch 6 from here on out) * dtr in next dtr, ch 6, Rep from *. End with sl st in fifth ch of ch-11 (16 sps).

Rnd 3: Ch 11, *dtr in next dtr, ch 6, rep from * 7 times, but at end of seventh time, do not ch 6. Ch 11, turn. This is where you will turn and work front, skipping sp where armhole will be. (8 dtr on this row.)

Rnd 4: Rep Row 3, ending with dtr in ch 5 of ch-11. Do not ch 11 at end of row. End off. (8 dtr)

Next Step: (space for armhole) Sk ch 6 sp to left of Row 3 (this will start back of sweater). See Diagram A.

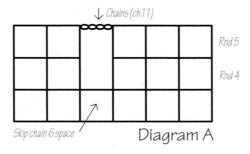

Diagram A

Rows 3-4 for back: Skipping ch-6 sp, join with sl st to next dtr, ch 11, and rep rows 3 and 4 same as front. This will leave a sp for armhole. At end of row 4 (after last dtr) do not end off yarn. Ch 11 (this ch-11 is space at bottom of

armhole sp), attach with sl st to ch 5 of ch 11 (of next corner), connecting to front of sweater. See Diagram B. End off. This will leave an armhole sp.

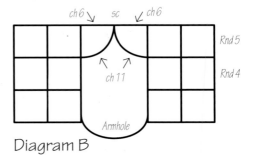

Diagram B

Next Step: At other side of sweater (at other side of Rnd 4), attach yarn with sl st to corner of ch-11, ch 11 again, and attach with sl st to next corner st on back, forming sp for armhole, the same as you did on the other side. Do not end off yarn. Proceed to Rnd 5.

Rnd 5: After sl st, ch 11, (dtr into next dtr, ch 6) 6 times, dtr in next dtr, ch 6, sc in ch 6 of ch-11 — See Diagram B for armhole — ch 6, dtr in next dtr, (ch 6, dtr in next dtr) 7 times, ch 6, sc in ch 6 of ch-11 (armhole), ch 6, sl st to ch 5 of ch-11 at beg of row (18 ch-6 sps).

Rnd 6: Ch 11, (dtr in next dtr, ch 6) 6 times.

Decrease Under Armhole: In these next 3 sts (dtr, sc and dtr), make dec this way: Work dtr in next dtr, leaving 2 lps on hook, dtr in sc, leaving 3 lps on hook, dtr in next dtr, leaving 4 lps on hook, yo and pull yarn through all 4 lps — 3 sts made into 1 st.

(Ch 6, dtr in next dtr) 6 times, ch 6. Make dec under underarm in this manner: dtr in next dtr, leaving 2 lps on hook dtr in sc, leaving 3 lps on hook, with 3 lps still on hook, sl st yarn into ch 5 of ch-11 (at beg of rnd). Now with 4 lps on hook, yo and pull yarn through

all lps on hook (dec made).

Rnd 7: Ch 11, dtr in next dtr (ch 6, dtr in next dtr) 12 times, ch 6, sl st to ch 5 of ch-11 (14 sps).

Rnd 8: Rep Rnd 7.

Rnd 9: * Ch 10, sl st in next dtr; rep from * around, end with ch 10 and sl st to first sl st. End off.

Sleeve
At either underarm, sl st yarn to sc.

Rnd 1: Ch 10, work 7 ch 5 sps, and 7 dtr evenly around armhole. Sl st to ch 5 of ch-10. (7 dtr and 7 ch-5-sps on this rnd.)

Rnd 2: Ch 10, dtr in next dtr, (ch 5, dtr in next dtr) 5 times. Ch 5, sl st to ch 5 of ch-10 (7 ch-5 sps).

Rnd 3 of sleeve: Rep Rnd 2, working ch 9 at beg, and ch 4 between each

dtr, instead of ch 10 at beg and ch 5 between (7 dtr and 7 ch-4 sps on rnd).

Rnds 4-6: Rep Rnd 3.

Rnds 7-8: Rep Rnd 2; end with sl st to ch 5 of ch-10. End off (ch 5 between each dtr).

Work other sleeve in the same manner. If sleeves are too short, add one more rnd.

Finishing: Neck Opening
Attach yarn to any dtr stitch. * Ch 4, sl st to next dtr. Rep from * around, end with sl st in first sl st. This will draw neck opening in to fit better. End off. If you want this to be an "off-the-shoulder" sweater, skip this step.

Skill Level — Intermediate

LIGHT
3
LEGER
Ligero

Fits sizes 2-3 (4-5), approx. chest size: 2-3 = 19"-21", 4-5 = 22"-24"

Toddler Capri Outfit

Make these adorable outfits for the little girls in your life, possibly in different colors. They will look so precious in the top and flared capri pants with rows of scalloped shells. If you wish, try adding sleeves or make the pants into shorts.

INSTRUCTIONS:
Ch 49 (53).

Row 1: 1 dc in third ch from hook and in each ch to end, turn — 48 (52) dc (tch counts as first dc).

Row 2: Ch 2, (counts as first dc throughout pattern) 1 dc in each dc to end, turn — 48 (52) dc.

Rows 3-4: Rep Row 2 — 48 (52) dc.

Shape Armholes
Row 5: Sl st over 4 dc, ch 2, dc in each dc to within last 4 dc. Leave last 4 dc unworked, turn — 40 (44) dc.

Row 6: Ch 2, work 2dctog (1 dec, see pg 9). Dc in next 36 (38) dc, work 2dc-tog, over last 2 dc, turn — 38 (42) dc.

Row 7: Ch 2, dec one dc at each end, turn — 36 (40) dc.

Row 8: Ch 2, dc in each dc across, turn — 36 (40) dc.

Shape Neck — Left Shoulder
Row 9: Ch 2, work dc in next 7 (7) dc, turn — 8 (8) dc.

Row 10: Ch 2, work 2dctog (dec) over first 2 dc, dc in rem dc, turn —7 (7) dc.

Row 11: Ch 2, dc in next 4 dc, 2dc-tog over last 2 dc, turn — 6 (6) dc.

Row 12: Ch 2, work 2dctog over first 2 dc, dc in each st to end, turn — 5 (5) dc.

Row 13: Work 1 dec at end of row (neck edge), turn — 4 (4) dc.

Row 14: Work 1 dec at beg of row. End off — 3 (3) dc.

Right Shoulder
With front of top facing you, attach yarn to eighth dc on unworked end of Row 9.

Row 9: Ch 2, dc in each of next 7 (7) dc, turn — 8 (8) dc.

Rows 10-14: Work rt shoulder to correspond with left shoulder, dec(ing) 1 on neck edge of top (Row 10 —7 (7) dc, Row 14 — 3 (3) dc). End off.

Back — Work Same as Front
Sew side seams tog with yarn and yarn needle using whip st.

Bottom Edge of Top
Pms at 17 (24) sts evenly spaced around bottom edge of top. Attach yarn in st at side seam. Ch 1, sc in same sp. Work 111 (126) sc evenly spaced around entire bottom edge, working 2 sc (inc) in each st where markers are placed. End off — 111 (126) sc.

Shell Rows
Work in rounds.

Rnd 1: With front of top facing you (upside down), pm at st where rt seam is. Attach yarn in seventh st to right of st where marker was placed. Sc in same place, * sk 6 sc, work 11 tr loosely in next st (at marker). Sk 6 sc, sc in next st; rep from *. End with sl st in first sc — 8 (9) tr shs.

Rnd 2: Ch 5 (counts as first tr), tr in same st, * ch 5, 1 sc into center tr on sh, ch 5, 2 tr in sc; rep from *. End with sl st in top of ch 5.

Rnd 3: Ch 1, * 1 sc between 2 tr, 11 tr in middle st of sh, rep from *. End with sl st in first sc.

Materials:
- 5 (6) balls (50 g/99 yd. each) light worsted-wt. yarn in lavender
- Size G/6 (4 mm) hook
- (4) 12" pieces lavender ribbon
- 14" (16") of ¼"-wide elastic for waist
- Sewing needle and matching thread
- Yarn needle

Used in this project: Queensland Collection Maldive yarn in lavendar

Gauge:
- 9 dc = 2"
- 11 dc rows = 4"
- 9 dc shell = 1¼"
- 11 dc shell = 2½"

Words of Encouragement
Sometimes we need to be careful about what we wish for. Some things we want can be good, but we need to listen to what we say. I know of a woman who was mad at her husband for not making enough money. She constantly belittled him and nagged for more money. Soon after that he died and left her with $250,000 in insurance money. She had plenty of money, but struggled terribly from the loss of someone she genuinely loved.

Rnds 4-9 (11): Rep Rnds 2 and 3 three (four) more times. End off. With needle and thread, sew four 12"-long pieces of ribbon to each shoulder.

Pants

Ch 98 (102), and join with sl st to make a circle, being careful not to twist ch.

Row 1: Ch 2 (count as first dc), 1 dc in each ch around. Join to top of ch 2, turn — 98 (102) dc.

Row 2: Ch 2, work 1 dc into front lp only of each dc to end, join, turn — 98 (102) dc.

Rows 3-18 (20): Rep Rnd 2, working sts into both lps on each rnd. End off.

Note: ½" will be taken up with fold over at top of pants where elastic is to be placed.

Separation for Legs

With pants lying flat, pm in center front st, and pm in center back st. Attach these 2 sts tog with marker or a piece of yarn, creating two leg openings. There will be 49 (51) sts on each side/leg.

Row 1 (of leg): Attach yarn to inside st of leg opening, ch 2, dc in same st (inc) dc in each dc around, join with sl st, turn — 50 (52) dc.

Row 2: Ch 2, inc 1 st at beg of row, work dc in each st around, join, turn — 51 (53) dc.

Row 3: Ch 2, work even with no inc, join, turn — 51 (53) dc.

Rows 4-11 (15): Rep Rows 2 and 3 — 55 (57) dc on Row 11 (15).

Row 12 (16): 8 (4) incs on this row: Pms in 8 (4) sts, evenly spaced on row 11 (15). Sc in each st around, working 2 sc (inc) in each st where marker is placed, join, turn — 63 (63) sc.

Row 13 (17): Ch 2, dc in next 4 dc, 2 dc in each of next 7 dc, * dc in next 4 dc, 2 dc in each of next 7 dc, rep from *; end with dc in each of last 7 dc, join with sl st. Do not turn — 98 (98) dc.

Shell Rows on Pants

Work in rnds.

Rnd 14 (18): Ch 1, sc in same sp as sl st, * sk 6 dc, 9 tr in next dc, sk 6 dc, sc in next dc; rep from *. End with sl st in first sc — 7 (7) shells.

Rnd 15 (19): Rep Rnd 2 of top under Shell Rows.

Rnd 16 (20): Rep Rnd 3 of top under Shell Rows — 7 (7) shells. End off. Rep Rows 1-16 (20) for other leg.

Note: If longer leg length is desired, rep Rnds 15 (19) and 16 (20).

Finishing

Fold first row of waist edge over to meet second row, and insert elastic holding securely with pins. Adjust to fit waist, and sew short ends of elastic tog, sl st folded edge to second row to secure elastic or sew with yarn and yarn needle. Weave in ends.

Finished size — 70" long

MEDIUM
4
MOYEN
Medio

Chain of Flowers Scarf

Simple chains and an easy pattern make this fun and funky neck garland a breeze. It can be worn many ways. The softness of the soy/wool yarn and variegated colors of this one-skein wonder make it a cool choice. You deserve to make one for yourself!

Materials:

1 skein (2.8 oz./80 g/ 110 yd.) soy/wool yarn in pink and tan

Size J/10 (6 mm) hook

Used in this project: Patons SWS yarn in Natural Geranium

Gauge:

10 chs = 3"

1 flower = 4¼" when flat

INSTRUCTIONS:

Rnd 1 of flower: Ch 3, * in second ch from hook, work 8 sc to form a ring, sl st to first sc — 8 sc.

Rnd 2: Ch 14, sl st in same sp (twice) * ch 14, sl st in next sc, ch 14, sl st in same sp, ch 14, sc in same sp, rep from * around, sl st to first sc — 16 ch lps.

Step 3: Ch 20, and rep from beg until you have 12 flowers. End off, and weave in ends.

Helpful Hint:

If you have set goals of being a designer, experience is good, but you don't have to be experienced to get your designs published. As long as your work looks good and your stitches are consistent, you are just as likely to get your designs published as someone who's been doing it for a long time. Try to keep up with fashion trends so you'll know what types of patterns are in demand.

Words of Encouragement

Do you only see faults in others and not in yourself? Do you ever feel that you can't get along with others, or think people don't want to be around you? Try to appreciate the positive qualities in people, and they will do their best to try and see your good traits. I have found that the two most important things that a person needs in this life are love and appreciation. Remember, "the times a person deserves our love and appreciation the least is really when they need it the most!"

Skill Level — Advanced Beginner

SUPER BULKY
6
SUPER BULKY
Super Abultado

Sizes — xs (sm, med, lg, xlg, 1x, 2x, 3x), all sizes 22" long

Airy Vest

If you're short on time, this is the project for you! Sometimes novelty yarns are difficult to work with because it's hard to see the stitches. The extra-large hook helps you to see the stitches, and the bulky yarn makes this vest work up super-fast for instant gratification. It's fitted and flattering — what more could you ask for?

Materials:

2 (2, 3, 3, 4, 4, 5, 5)
skeins (4 oz./113 g/
89 yd.) yarn in blue/green

Size Q (16 mm) hook

2 yd. 1½" brown ribbon

Yarn needle

*Used in this project: Yarn
Bee Artistry Yarn in Monet
(from Hobby Lobby)*

Gauge:

4 dc = 3¾"

3 dc rows = 4" (since
there are sps between
the dcs, be sure and
measure from the center
of the sps and not from
the edge of the dcs)

INSTRUCTIONS:

The vest is made in one piece up to
the bottom of armholes, and then
each front and back are added and
joined at the shoulders.

Row 1: Ch 35 (37, 39, 41, 43, 45,
47, 49), dc in fourth ch from hook and
in each ch across, ch 3, turn — 33
(35, 37, 39, 41, 43, 45, 47) dc.

Row 2: Dc in each dc across, ch 3,
turn — 33 (35, 37, 39, 41, 43, 45,
47) dc.

Rows 3-10: Rep Row 2, ch 3 and
turn each row. Do not end off.

Left Front

Row 1: Ch 3 (counts as first dc), dc
in next 6 (6, 7, 7, 8, 8, 9, 9) dc, ch 3,
turn — 7 (7, 8, 8, 9, 9, 10, 10) dc and
6 (6, 7, 7, 8, 8, 9, 9) sps.

Row 2: Dc in next 4 (4, 5, 5, 6, 6, 7,
7), work 2 dc tog (1 dc dec, see pg.
9) in last 2 dc, ch 3, turn — 6 (6, 7, 7,
8, 8, 9, 9) dc.

Row 3: Work even with no decs.

Row 4: Dec 1 dc at beg of row as in
Row 2, ch 3, turn — 5 (5, 6, 6, 7, 7,
8, 8) dc.

Row 5: Work even with no decs.
End off.

Right Front

Turn vest to inside, attach yarn to
unworked end of Row 10 at top of dc
at corner on opposite side of front,
and rep Rows 1-5 of left front.

Back

Row 1: Sk 4 (4, 4, 5, 5, 5, 6, 6) sps
for armhole, attach yarn to next dc, ch
3, dc in next 11 (13, 13, 13, 13, 15,
13, 15) dc, ch 3, turn —12 (14, 14,
14, 14, 16, 14, 16) dc, 11 (13, 13,
13, 13, 15, 13, 15) sps.

Rows 2-5: Work even. End off after
Row 5.

Sew shoulder seams, weave ribbon
through sps, and tie into a bow in front.

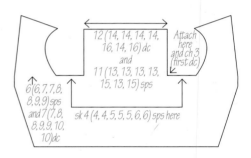

*Optional button closure (instead of ribbon):
Sew button on one side at front opening.
To make a lp: Attach yarn to other edge of
front, make a ch long enough to go around
button and make a lp by attaching to same
sp where attached.*

Words of Encouragement

*Instant gratification has is own magnetism, but we need to take the time to stop and think
about the consequences of an action. There are some people in this world who do not seem to
have a conscience, and they usually have a difficult life. I heard a statement once that I really
agree with: "Some people have amnesia to consequences." Practicing being alert to unwanted
consequences helps with life's climate control, preventing unnecessary storms.*

Helpful Hint:
*There is no RS or WS
to this vest, making it
reversible.*

120

MEDIUM
4
MOYEN
Medio

SUPER BULKY
6
SUPER BULKY
Super Abultado

Fits girls' sizes 1-3 (6¾" long) and 4-6 (8¾" long), and adult x-sm (sm, med, lg, xlg, 1x)
Finished length (adult) — 9½"

Soft Capelets

These pretty Victorian-style capelets are easy to make because they have no increases or decreases. A decorative shell edge tops it off! Make them for your daughters, granddaughters or nieces, and snap a photo they will cherish forever.

Materials:

2 (2, 2, 3, 3, 3) skeins (2.8 oz./80 g/68 yd. each) chenille-type yarn in variegated pinks, blues and purples (1 skein for girls' sizes 1-3, 2 skeins for girls sizes 4-6)

1 skein (5 oz./260 yd.) yarn for shell trim (CC)

Size N/15 (10 mm) and K/10.5 (6.5 mm) hooks

2 yd. 1½" clear ribbon (1⅓ yd. for girl's size)

Used in this project: Patons Bohemian yarn #6, extra-bulky in Poetic Pinks, TLC Heathers #4 in Mulberry.

Gauge:

3 sc (chs between) 2½"

5 sc rows = 3"

1 5dc Shell=1¾"

Helpful Hint:

If a longer capelet is desired, make extra chs in increments of four.

INSTRUCTIONS:
Adult Capelet
Work from side to side.

Row 1: Ch 18 (18, 22, 22, 26, 26), sc in second ch from hook, * ch 1, sc in next ch; rep from * across row, ch 1, turn — 9 (9, 11, 11, 13, 13) sc and 8 (8, 10, 10, 12, 12) ch-1 sps.

Row 2: * Sc in next sc, ch 1; rep from * across, sc in last sc, ch 1, turn.

Rows 3-58 (62, 66, 70, 74, 78): Rep Row 2. End off after last row. Work more rows in increments of 4 for a wider capelet. At this point, capelet should measure 34" (36¼", 38½", 40¾", 43", 45¼") wide and 8½" (8½", 10¼", 10¼", 12", 12") long.

Top Edge for Ribbon
Work loose dcs.

At top rt neck edge, attach yarn to sc at corner, ch 3, * sk next row, dc in end of next row, rep from * across. End off — 30 (32, 34, 36, 38, 40) dc and 29 (31, 33, 35, 37, 39) sps.

Shell Edging
Change to K hook.

Starting at left neck edge and with front facing, attach CC to corner (top of dc). Ch 1, sc in same sp, sk horizontal dc (5-dc sh in next sc, sk next st, sc in next st, sk next st), 4 (4, 5, 5, 6, 6) times. You should have 4 (4, 5, 5, 6, 6) sh(s) on side edge. Continuing around, 7-dc sh in corner, * sk next st, sc in next st, sk next st, 5-dc sh in next st. Rep from * along bottom edge, and 7-dc sh in next corner. Work side edge as before, and end with sc in corner — 18 (19, 20, 21, 22, 23) evenly spaced shs on bottom edge — 28 (29, 30, 31, 32, 33) total shs.

Girl's Capelet — Sizes 1-3 (4-6)
Work from side to side.

Row 1: Ch 12 (16) sc in second ch from hook, * ch 1, sk next ch, sc in next ch; rep from * across row, ch 1, turn — 6 (8) sc and 5 (7) ch-1 sps.

Row 2: * Sc in next sc, ch 1; rep from * across, sc in last sc, ch 1, turn.

Rows 3-34 (48): Rep Row 2, ending off after last row. Work more rows in increments of 4 for a wider capelet.

Top Edge for Ribbon
Work top edge same as adult capelet. At end you will have 18 (25) dc and 17 (24) sps.

Shell Edging — First Side Edge
Attach CC in corner st at top of last dc just worked, ch 1, sc in same sp, work 5 dc sh around post of dc, * sc in next sc, sk next ch-1, 5 dc sh in next sc, skip next ch-1; rep from * 1 (2) more times, sc in next sc, sk next st — 3 (4) shells on side edge, excluding corner. Cont working along bottom edge same as adult capelet, starting with 7 dc sh in corner. Work up other side same as before, ending with last sh around post of dc; sc in corner on top edge. End off — 10 (11) shells on bottom edge, 18 (21) shells total.

Finishing – All Sizes
Weave in ends. Cut ends of ribbon at a slant and weave through dcs at neck edge, starting at corner.

Words of Encouragement

Are you under a lot of stress? Do you sometimes feel that you are headed toward the edge? By all means, seek out someone to talk to. Reach out to people so they will know you need them, and you will not have to go through difficult times alone.

Finished size — Women's 5-6 (7-8, 9-11)

Skill Level — Advanced Beginner

MEDIUM
4
MOYEN
Medio

BULKY
5
BULKY
Abultado

Mary Jane Slippers

These slippers will feel warm and cozy on a snowy winter night. Using novelty yarns, such as loopy bouclé or fun fur, can be challenging; you have to "feel" the stitches, and sometimes it is easier to use another plain yarn along with the loopy yarn. If you get frustrated, don't give up! Take a deep breath, and keep trying.

Materials:

1 skein (6 oz./170 g/ 185 yd.) bulky yarn in red (A)

1 skein (3.5 oz./198 yd.) medium worsted-weight yarn in red (B)

1 skein (3.5 oz./198 yd.) medium worsted-weight yarn in black (C)

Size K/10.5 (6.5 mm) hook

2 black ½" snaps

2 black ⅝" buttons

Yarn needle

Sewing needle and black thread

Used in this project: Lion Brand Homespun yarn in Candy Apple Red, Red Heart yarn in Cherry Red and Bernat Super Value yarn in black.

Gauge:

1 sc = ½"

2 sc rows = ¾"

Helpful Hint:

You can make these slippers smaller (for a toddler) or larger (for a man) by working less or more scs in rnds at beg and by working less or more rows after you have divided the rnds to work sides and soles.

INSTRUCTIONS:
Make 2.

With 2 strands worked tog (A and B) ch 4, join to first ch to form a ring.

Rnd 1: Marking first sc at beg of each rnd, work 10 sc in ring, join to first sc — 10 sc.

Rnd 2: * 2 sc in next sc, 1 sc in next sc, rep from * cont to work in rnds, working past the marker, until you have 20 (20, 22) sts for toe. For extra-wide feet, work 2 sts more per size. Cont working scs with no incs without joining rnds, until work measures 3½" (3½", 4"). Do not end off.

Divide for Sides and Sole
Row 1: Ch 1, turn. Work sc in each of next 12 (12, 13) sts.

Note: Add 2 more sts here if you are making slippers for extra wide feet.

Next Row: Rep Row 1 — 12 (12,13) sts.

Cont working sides and sole of slipper in this manner with 12 (12, 13) sc on each row until piece is 5-1/2" (6", 7") measured from Row 1 of sides and sole or to desired length. End off. With rt sides tog, sew heel seam with yarn and yarn needle. Adjust to fit if necessary.

Top Edge — Wedge at heel
All sizes — A + B held tog.

To form wedg at heel: Count over 9 sts to left from center back seam of heel and pm. Count over 9 sts to rt of seam and pm. You will build up a wedge at heel between these 2 markers. Join yarn to st at marker on rt side of shoe, sk next st, sc in each of next 15 sts, sk next st, sl st in next st (at marker). End off.

Next Step: Join yarn to back center seam, and work scs all around. Dec 1 sc (2sctog, see pg. 9) at beg of row, 1 sc dec at end of row, 1 dec on each side where markers were placed, and 1 dec at each corner on top of slipper. End off — 6 dec.

Straps
A + B held tog.

For left foot, attach yarn to rt of st where marker was placed on RS of slipper. For right foot, join yarn on opp side of second slipper. Ch 13 (13, 15), turn, sc in second ch from hook and in each ch across. Sl st to edge of slipper. End off — 12 (12, 14) sc.

Trim
Using 1 strand of black yarn (C), attach to center st at top edge of heel, sc in same sp, sc in each st around top edge of slipper and strap, working 2 sc in each of the 3 sc on end of strap to prevent curling. End off.

Finishing
Weave in ends. Sew snaps to underside of strap and side of slipper. Sew button to top of strap end.

Words of Encouragement
When life is challenging and trials and adversities come up, just hang in there and keep trying. The storms of life help build character, and we often learn and grow most from our difficulties and hardships. The important thing in life is not what happens to you, but what you are becoming as a result. Someone pointed out that a sculptor uses soft polishing cloths along with hammers and chisels. The polishing cloth feels smooth, but it is the hammer and chisel that carves the distinct lines of true beauty and character. Persevere and believe, for God is at work on a masterpiece.

Yarn Companies

I want to thank all the yarn companies who so generously supplied yarn for the designs in this book.

Bernat, Patons and Lily Yarns
P. O. Box 40
Listowel, Ontario, Canada N4W 3H3
www.bernat.com
www.patonsyarns.com
www.lilyyarns.com

Berroco, Inc.
(Used in sweater on front cover)
P. O. Box 367
14 Elmdale Rd.
Uxbridge, MA 01569
www.berroco.com

Caron International
1481 W. 2nd St.
Washington, NC 27889
www.caron.com

Coats & Clark
P.O. Box 12229
Greenville, SC 29612-0229
(800) 648-1479
www.coatsandclark.com

Hobby Lobby Stores, Inc.
(Yarn Bee Yarns)
7707 SW 44th St.
Oklahoma City, OK 73179
www.hobbylobby.com
www.craftsetc.com

Knitting Fever, Inc.
35 Debevoise Ave.
Roosevelt, NY 11575
(516) 546-3600
www.knittingfever.com

Lion Brand
34 W. 15th St.
New York, NY 10011
(800) 258-9276
www.lionbrand.com

OTHER RESOURCES

Michael's Craft Stores
8000 Bent Branch Dr.
Irving, TX 75063
(800) 642-4235
www.michaels.com

JoAnn Fabrics and Crafts
5555 Darrow Road
Hudson, OH 44236
(330) 656-2600
www.joann.com

Hancock Fabrics
One Fashion Way
Baldwyn, Mississippi 38824
(877) 322-7427
www.hancockfabrics.com

Crochet Style ETC
(for Hilos Omega nylon crochet cord in 74 colors and Sinfonia cotton yarn)
http://crochetstyleetc.com

About the Author

Mary Jane Hall is originally from Texas and currently lives in Ohio. She has been married for 36 years, and she and her husband, Terry, have three grown children who are all married and have families of their own. They enjoy their grandchildren, who are a huge part of their lives. Mary Jane manages a "free" clothing store, called United Voluntary Services, which clothes more than 1,500 people in their county every year.

Mary Jane has a background in graphic design, color analysis, and real estate. She has spoken to many women's groups on positive living, including marriage and family relationships. An avid singer, Mary Jane has given concerts at fairs, festivals and many other events for much of her life. She also has had many TV and radio appearances and recorded an album in the 90s.

Mary Jane has been crocheting for 37 years and has taught more than 60 people how to crochet. She has given talks on "How to Get Published" and "Designing Tips" to local crochet groups, including the Crochet Guild of America, Dayton, Ohio, chapter.

Mary Jane specializes in crochet fashion design, and she is a Professional member of the National Crochet Guild of America (CGOA). Mary Jane is passionate about crochet and loves designing trendy wearables. She has had many of her original designs published in various books and magazines, and she designs full-time. Visit Mary Jane's Web site at www.mjcrochet.com.

Life and Crochet

Life is an intricate pattern, a myriad of stitches, woven one day at a time. We anxiously begin our design with a chain of good intentions, dreaming of the product yet to evolve. In the beginning we are full of tension, creating needless wasted energy. As we learn to relax, we feel a surprising tranquility needed to acquire the joy for the journey.

Life is wonderful until we hit a snag or a knot along the way. We struggle and fight. Then we realize we must slowly work through problems and sometimes have to start over. We want to quit, but we pick ourselves up and continue, realizing that mistakes teach us patience, and patience brings about worthwhile satisfaction. Sometimes we forget or refuse to ask for help, and we find ourselves decreasing, when we should be increasing in our abilities.

Yes, life is an intricate and sometimes difficult pattern with roadblocks along the way. But we must have faith and belief that when worked with determination and confidence, the end result will be heavenly!

— Judy Drewett

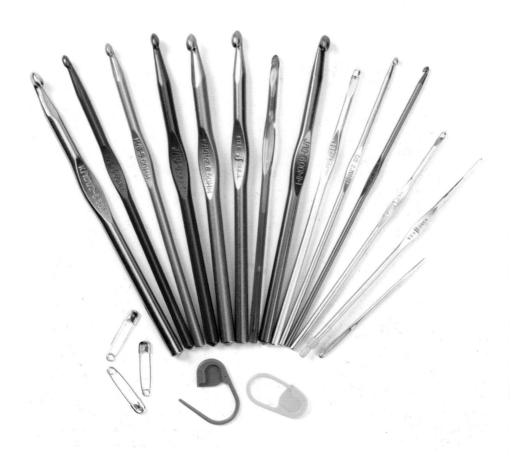

LEARN TO CROSS, TWIST, AND DROP
YOUR WAY TO CROCHET SUCCESS

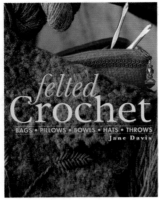

Felted Crochet
by Jane Davis

This resource provides step-by-step instructions for easily creating 30 beautiful accents for home and wardrobe, including purses, bags, blankets, vets, pillows and more.

Softcover • 8¼ x 10⅞ • 128 pages
125 color photos and illus.
Item# FELCR • $22.99

Easy to Crochet Cute Clothes For Kids
by Sue Whiting

Explore the versatility of crochet as you create 25 easy outfits and accessories for babies and toddlers, using a variety of contemporary yarns.

Softcover • 10 x 8¼ • 128 pages
75 color photos & illus.
Item# Z1439 • $19.99

Easy Crocheted Accessories
by Carol Meldrum

Create 20 chic crocheted items including bags, ponchos, scarves, throws and gloves with the guidance of detailed instructions and 200 brilliant color photos.

Softcover • 7½ x 9¾ • 128 pages
200 color photos
Item# ECA • $24.99

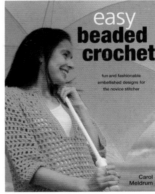

Easy Beaded Crochet
Fun and Fashionable Embellished Designs for the Novice Stitcher
by Carol Meldrum

Create more than 20 embellished garments and accessories including a lace-effect shawl, vintage scarf and funky bag using techniques demonstrated in 200 color photos and illustrations.

Softcover • 7½ x 9½ • 128 pages
200 color photos, illus.
Item# Z0221 • $24.99

Single Crochet for Beginners
by Cindy Crandall-Frazier

Create more than 30 fun projects with a single crochet stitch using this simple guide! Step-by-step instructions and a quick guide to color and fabric give you the details to create beautiful projects for your home or wardrobe.

Softcover • 8 x 8 w/flaps • 160 pages
125 color photos and illus.
Item# SGLCR • $22.99